The Research Paper
and the
World Wide Web

The Research Paper
and the
World Wide Web

SECOND EDITION

Dawn Rodrigues

*University of Texas at Brownsville/
Texas Southmost College*

Raymond J. Rodrigues

*University of Texas at Brownsville/
Texas Southmost College*

PRENTICE HALL
Upper Saddle River, NJ 07458

Library of Congress Cataloging-in-Publication Data

Rodrigues, Dawn.
    The research paper and the World Wide Web / Dawn Rodrigues,
Raymond Rodrigues. — 2nd ed.
        p.   cm.
    Includes bibliographical references (p. 173) and index.
    ISBN 0-13-021020-X
    1. Research—Data processing.   2. World Wide Web (Information
retrieval system)   3. Internet (Computer network) in education.
I. Rodrigues, Raymond J., 1938–   II. Title.
    LB2369.R585   2000
    808'.027—dc21   99-35189
                                                        CIP

Editorial Director: Charlyce Jones-Owen
Editor-in-Chief: Leah Jewell
Assistant Editor: Vivian Garcia
Editorial Assistant: Patricia Castiglione
Managing Editor: Bonnie Biller
Production Liaison: Fran Russello
Project Manager: Stratford Publishing Services
Prepress and Manufacturing Buyer: Mary Ann Gloriande
Art Director: Jane Conte
Cover Designer: Maureen Eide
Cover Art: Coco Musada
Marketing Manager: Sue Brekka
Copyeditor: David Lee Prout

This book was set in 10/12 Palatino by Stratford Publishing Services, Inc.
and was printed and bound by Courier Companies, Inc. The cover was printed by
Phoenix Color Corp.

© 2000, 1997 by Prentice-Hall, Inc.
Upper Saddle River, NJ 07458

Printed in the United States of America
10 9 8 7 6 5 4 3 2 1

ISBN 0-13-021020-X

Prentice-Hall International (UK) Limited, London
Prentice-Hall of Australia Pty. Limited, Sydney
Prentice-Hall Canada Inc., Toronto
Prentice-Hall Hispanoamericana, S.A., Mexico
Prentice-Hall of India Private Limited, New Delhi
Prentice-Hall of Japan, Inc., Tokyo
Pearson Education Asia Pte. Ltd., Singapore
Editora Prentice-Hall do Brasil, Ltda., Rio de Janeiro

Contents

Preface

We have designed this book to serve several different types of readers. First are those readers who may be starting to learn how to develop research papers and who need to learn how to conduct research in libraries and online through the World Wide Web. Second are those who know how to do traditional library research, but who have not yet learned how to use the Web as a major source of research. And third are those who may have begun exploring the Web, but who have not yet mastered the Web as a research tool. As a result, this book can serve as a stand-alone guide to writing research papers, or it can serve as a guide on how to integrate the research now available on the Web with the research that has always been possible through library research.

As a student or a professional involved in writing research papers or reports, you may have already begun to use technology as a tool for information gathering. You may have even used the World Wide Web for research or used online databases for information gathering. But chances are that you still have unanswered questions about such topics as which search engines are best for which types of research, how to validate sources, how to search more efficiently, or how to organize the information that you find so that you can, at some point, incorporate it into a research paper or project report.

This book will help you learn how to locate answers to your questions as you learn how to integrate Web searching with library searching. Beginning with a discussion of the research process, early chapters help you learn how to adapt your research process to the information age, moving between Web and library as appropriate, locating sources in your discipline, even doing e-mail or listserv research along the way. A later chapter explains how to use bookmarks to organize your notes from electronic sources, and the final chapter presents proper documentation style in your paper.

How the Chapters and the Book Are Organized

Each chapter begins with the major goals that the chapter is designed to help you learn. Within each chapter, there are Practice Boxes with exercises based upon the material that has immediately preceded them, usually asking you to apply a specific technique and suggesting ways that you can share what you learn with your classmates. At the end of each chapter is a set of exercises designed to lead you through the processes of developing research topics, finding and validating sources, organizing notes, and citing sources appropriately, while writing drafts of the research paper. For your convenience, inside the back cover we have outlined the process of writing a research paper and referred to the places in the book where the relevant skills are to be found. Finally, for those of you who may be seeking research topics about research processes themselves or how they may be used among various professions, we suggest some topics in Chapter 1.

Ideally, you will do two types of research projects while reading through this book: (1) projects in which your focus is more on learning the processes of research than on doing an extensive examination of a topic and (2) a formal research paper for which you have been prepared by moving through all the chapters of the book. If circumstances require you to read this book both to learn research techniques and to do a research project at the same time, you may need to move backward and forward in the book as needed, reading chapters that are most useful to you at any given point in your research process. Here, the guide inside the back cover can help.

In the first chapter you learn the basics of the research process, allowing you to begin work on your research paper before reading subsequent chapters.

The second chapter focuses on library Web searching, so that you can learn how to incorporate the Web into your traditional research process. It also discusses how to use the library and traditional library resources.

The third chapter focuses on the kinds of library and Web resources accessible through the Web. You continue to learn how to integrate library searching with Internet searching.

The fourth chapter, "Finding Resources in the Disciplines", discusses specific Web sources designed for specific disciplines, because knowing their availability may make your search processes more efficient.

The fifth chapter on evaluating sources deals with ways of determining how valuable the sources you find on the Web—and in libraries—may be. There is no shortage of research sources, but some are worth using more than others.

The sixth chapter guides you through the techniques of using other Web tools that researchers may at first overlook: e-mail, listservs, focus groups, and newsgroups.

The seventh chapter on note taking is designed to make your research more efficient and better organized so that, when it is time to draft your research paper, you are ready.

The eighth chapter explains how to document online sources and cite them properly. Equally important, the chapter reviews how and when to summarize, to paraphrase, and to quote sources. It includes a sample research paper as a model.

Acknowledgements

First, we would like to thank the reviewers, Nancy S. Tucker Ph. D., Michigan State University; Nancy A. Barta-Smith, Slippery Rock University; and Joy Chase, Evergreen Valley College; for their numerous helpful suggestions.

Next, we want to thank our son, Brad, for his encouragement and advice. we couldn't have completed a task like this without his support. Finally, we'd like to say how much we've appreciated the supportive and warm working relationship we've had with our associates at Prentice Hall: Leah Jewell, Vivian Garcia, Linda Demasi, Fran Russello, and Patricia Castiglione.

The Research Paper
and the
World Wide Web

The Research Process in the Information Age

After completing this chapter, you should be able to do the following:

■ Select a topic for a research project.

■ Visit your library and become familiar with the basic strategies of using a library, including how to check out a book and how to locate a library database

■ Learn how to use the Web sufficiently so that you can do preliminary Web searching on your topic.

■ Do background reading on your topic in the library and on the Web.

■ Establish research questions.

■ Develop a research agenda.

THE RESEARCH PAPER IN THE INFORMATION AGE

Writing a research paper or report used to mean spending hours on end in a library, wading through card catalogs and taking notes from whatever books and journals were available to you. With vast resources of information having moved outside library walls and onto the World Wide Web, research and writing processes are changing. Clearly, research that excludes the Web and other online resources is not comprehensive research. Not only library collections but also online databases and periodical indexes are accessible through the Web.

Before the Web was a reality, the topics students could select for research were limited to the sources available in their own institution's library or to the books they might reasonably expect to get through interlibrary loan. If, for example, you wanted to do a research paper on Hispanic folklore, you might not have found more than a few books on the topic in your library. But with the Internet, you have access to many Web resources developed by scholars at colleges and universities across the nation and around the world. You also have access to libraries worldwide: you can search their collections, locate the material you need, and then order it through the interlibrary loan services at your institution.

The Web offers other new possibilities:

■ You can locate experts on your topic and conduct e-mail interviews with them.
■ You can determine what people think about your topic by searching newsgroup through dejanews.
■ You can discuss ideas and collaborate with colleagues in chat groups, listservs, or forums (see Chapter 6).

If you use the Web and online databases extensively for your research, your research process is likely to change. In the dynamic environment of the Web, research becomes a dialogical process: you interact with databases and the results change your understanding of your topic; or you interact with other students or researchers, and their responses help shape your views. A reference that you find using a search engine may cause you to shift the direction of your search; a note from a colleague on e-mail or a response to a posting on a newsgroup (see Chapter 6) might cause you to reexamine your topic or to think of new angles for your investigation.

THE RESEARCH AND WRITING PROCESS

This chapter provides you with suggestions for moving through the research process and offers advice for integrating library and Web searching throughout your research and writing process. You can also find resources on the Web to help you with research writing. Here are a few useful sites:

Cornell University Library, Library Research: A Hypertext Guide
http://urisref.library.cornell.edu

Oregon State University, Library Research Process Home Page
http://www.orst.edu/dept/library/tutorial/library.htm

University of California–Santa Cruz, Using the Web for Research: Tutorial
http://bob.ucsc.edu/library/media/research.html

To locate other sites for tutorials, go to a search engine such as Alta Vista, Lycos, or Infoseek, and type in a search phrase such as "library research tutorial" or "research tutorial," for new ones are being added regularly.

Establish a Topic or Research Project by Reading and Searching

Don't begin by finding a topic or selecting a research project at random. Rather, begin by thinking about a range of possibilities and delaying your selection of a specific topic or a project until after you've done preliminary searching and reading.

Your research project should be meaningful to you personally, whether it is assigned by a teacher or self-generated. If you select a topic that you *want* to investigate critically, then you are certain to benefit from the research process. If you customize and personalize assigned topics, you will enjoy your research. If you incorporate the Web and online database searching into your research process, you will have the added satisfaction of developing important information age literacies while completing your required assignment.

You can begin to determine your research topic in many ways: you can read encyclopedia entries, you can search for Web sources, you can explore library catalogs, you can talk with your friends face-to-face, or you can chat with people from around the world in an online chat area. Take your time. As Ken Macrorie says in *Searching Writing* (1980), it is better to let a topic find you than to settle on a topic just because you have to write a paper. Even if you have a more narrow topic already assigned as part of a class, there are probably many ways to define the topic, narrow it further, and arrive at some aspect of the topic that truly interests you.

Browsing versus Searching

Instead of searching—an active process in which you are looking for specific kinds of sources—begin by "browsing," exploring casually, with an open mind. Use subject-area directories such as those available at Yahoo! <hhttp://www.yahoo.com> or Galaxy <http://galaxy.einet.net/>. Although these sites have search engines available for you to explore the entire Web, these subject collections feature sites that people have collected and organized into categories. When you don't yet know a specific topic, you should consider beginning your research by browsing for information rather than searching for specific topics. By browsing, you see a range of possibilities, and you have a chance to consider many aspects of the topic you are examining.

Explore the Web to see what is available and to get a sense of what businesses are doing and publishing. The page in Figure 1.1 is one of many pages that can be located through a simple Web search for "electronic commerce."

Even though you might give the page a low evaluation—since it is filled with popular articles, not scholarly ones—nonetheless, it may yield some insights. If so, you can take notes.

Browse through library catalogs to get a sense of the possibilities. Read through the list of books available at the Rutgers Library in Figure 1.2 and notice how, just by reading titles, you are able to come up with several topic possibilities for a research project. Of course, when you begin reading your sources, you will have an increased sense of the possibilities.

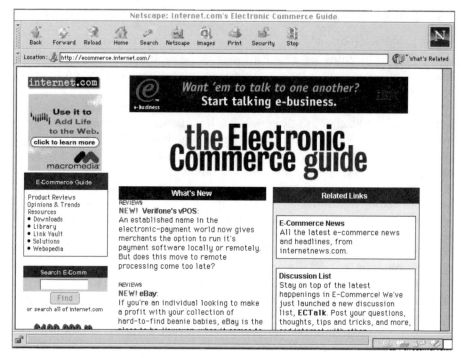

FIGURE 1.1   E-commerce Web site.

Skimming versus Reading

As you locate possible ideas, skim through the sources, allowing topic possibilities to percolate in the back of your mind. As you pour through a range of sources, you will gradually gain a sense of what interests you, and you will develop a sense of what has been said about your topic by others. Here are some questions to guide you as you browse and skim sources:

- What are the restrictions on my topic? What is the range of possibilities?
- What standard library sources should I consult?
- How can a reference librarian help me?
- What library resources should I consult?
- Is this a Web-intensive kind of project? (Recent topics such as immigration reform, affirmative action, current events, etc., might be more appropriate for Web searching than a library search.)
- Are there any Web collections of resources on the topic that have been assembled by others (sometimes called "pathfinder sites")?
- What aspects of my research topic are especially intriguing?
- What do I know already about my topic?
- What do I need to learn?

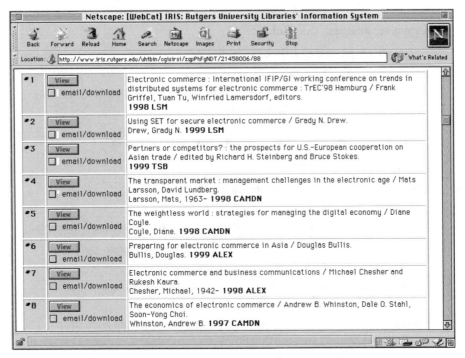

FIGURE 1.2 Books on E-commerce in Rutgers Library.

Establish Research Questions

Research is the exploration and investigation of a question or set of questions you want to know more about. You will take your work more seriously if you first formulate research questions, regardless of whether the research is an exploration of technology use in schools and colleges, an investigation of the North American Free Trade Agreement (NAFTA), an examination of the complex of issues surrounding various cancer treatments, or an inquiry into the latest methods of teaching reading.

Using the Web as a key tool or as a part of your research process, you need to go through the same basic steps researchers have gone through for ages. Begin by establishing research questions to help clarify your topic and to direct your research process. By "research questions," we mean the answers to the questions "What do you really want to know about your topic?", "What is really worth learning?", not "What is the topic?". Taking time to select and identify a research question helps turn even a dull writing assignment or research project into a meaningful and perhaps exciting one. The following box includes some suggestions for developing your research questions.

Developing Research Questions

1. State your topic as a question.

   Topic: Technology in Colleges and Universities
   Question: What are the most cost-effective ways to incorporate technology into college instruction?

   Topic: The North American Free Trade Agreement
   Question: What are the strengths and weaknesses of NAFTA?

2. Pose several sub-questions.

   Topic: Technology in Colleges and Universities
   Subquestions:

   What kinds of opposition to technology use can be expected from students?

   What opposition to integrating technology into the curriculum can be expected from faculty?

   Can effective use of Internet research address some of the opposition to using technology in the curriculum?

   What methods of integrating technology into the curriculum have been demonstrated to be productive nationally?

   Topic: The North American Free Trade Agreement
   Subquestions:

   Has the North American Free Trade Agreement taken jobs away from our citizens?

   What industries have grown or decreased in our country as a result of NAFTA?

   What danger to trade might exist if Mexico decides to increase taxes on the maquiladoras?

   Are maquiladoras environmentally safe?

Sample Research Questions

Below are samples of good research questions on a couple of topics, including "technology in the schools" and "the North American Free Trade Agreement."

1. **How has the North American Free Trade Agreement affected industry and business in the United States?** Find out what some of the factors are that can cause industry or business to decline as a result of NAFTA. Is there any direct proof that NAFTA has harmed or helped industry and business in the United States? What organizations measure the effects of NAFTA? Are all of the measures equally objective, or are some reported with a particular political bias? Has NAFTA affected

all parts of the nation equally? What caused some industries to grow, while others have declined as a result of NAFTA?

Possible methods for answering preliminary questions:

—Interview business or industry leaders in your community or region.
—Locate descriptions of NAFTA, including the laws and regulations that define NAFTA.
—Search your library catalog for possible sources.
—Search government documents for policies, regulations, and laws.
—Use Web search tools to do Web research on maquiladoras, community economic development council reports, or university research centers that study NAFTA and other sites that explore aspects of NAFTA.
—Join a listserv that discusses NAFTA-related topics.

2. **To what extent is technology changing instruction on campuses across the nation?** What is driving the use of technology: a desire to improve instruction or a dream of saving money? Are students satisfied with their access to computers on your campus? How does your campus compare to other campuses with regard to technology use? Are students encouraged to create their own home pages? Do students on your campus who come from secondary schools with high tech environments have a decided advantage over other students? Do faculty who use computing technology teach differently or better than they would without the technology, or have they simply transferred traditional lectures to the technology? What factors determine whether technology is used effectively?

Possible methods for answering preliminary questions:

—Interview professors who use technology in teaching.
—Use e-mail to interview students who have taken computer-intensive courses.
—Find our if your college or university offers distance learning. If so, learn as much as you can about how these courses are conducted.
—Read different articles presenting different views of the technology integration topic and note what the key questions seem to be (e.g., *Educom Review* <http://www.educom.com>; *Syllabus* <http://syllabus. com>).
—Do a web search on the topic.
—Join the American Association of Higher Education's discussion list on technology to tune in to the kinds of issues that interest university professors and administrators.

Plan Research Methodologies

After you have established your research questions, you will be in a better position to determine what research methods are appropriate to your topic. You may need to combine library searching with interviewing, conducting experiments, developing surveys, or observing behavior in research sites. In all cases, however, you will need to do at least some library and Web searching to learn more about your topic or what research they have conducted in the general area.

Some of your research strategies will be driven by the expectations of your field. Even if you are in a freshmen level course, you may want to learn more about the expectations that professors in specific disciplines would have for a paper on your topic. If, for example, your paper is on affirmative action, you can learn how sociologists conduct and report research. If you wish, you can build learning about research in a specific discipline into your research agenda. Not only will you have gained expertise about a specific topic, but you also will have oriented yourself to the conventions and ways of thinking that are characteristic of your discipline. (See Chapter 4 for guidance on tailoring research to specific disciplines.)

After doing some preliminary browsing and searching, decide which Web search tools and references you will use for the balance of your research and which library catalogs you plan to explore. In addition, think about how you'll organize your search results. (Chapter 7 explains how to use bookmarks and file structures to organize your notes.)

Identify Keywords through Research Questions

Develop a list of keywords or "descriptors"—words that describe your topic and that are likely to have been used in titles or abstracts of the book and journals you are exploring. Continually revise this list. It is a good idea to search a variety of databases using the same terms, expanding your list of keywords as you find new keywords or cross-references. When the database you are searching suggests that you "see also" several other topics, review the findings and note whether any additional key words look promising. If so, see what kinds of results you get when you change the search terms.

If you begin your research with library card catalogs, you should consult the *Library of Congress Subject Headings* to help you develop your list of keywords. Libraries use a standard set of terms to categorize their holdings. *The Library of Congress Subject Headings,* four bound volumes containing lists of these terms, is usually located near a library's reference desk. An online method of finding correct headings is to find one book or journal on your topic by doing either an author or a title search. When you display the full record, you can see what subject headings have been assigned to your topic.

If you begin your research on the Web, you will need to use keywords that correspond to main concepts or to topics that you would expect to find in your sources. Unlike the Library of Congress, the Web uses no standardized set of keywords; nonetheless, you can use many of the same keywords for both library and Web searching. If you start your search with the Web, try using the words that come naturally to you when you talk about a given topic.

After you see your results, you'll know whether you need to narrow or broaden your search. In many library catalogs and on most Web sites, you can do some Boolean searching, which allows you to use AND, OR, and NOT to define the conditions of your search. (George Boole was an English mathematician who developed ways of describing the contents of mathematical sets by using AND, OR, and NOT.) If you search for information on affirmative action using Boolean operators, you would be able to search in the following ways:

- **Affirmative OR action**—This combination would give you all the information that uses the term *affirmative* or the term *action*; this would not be a good idea. You typically use OR with synonyms or related concepts, as in the next example.
- **Affirmative action OR diversity**—This list of words would give you all the information that uses the term *affirmative action* along with the information that uses the term *diversity*. You are likely to get a large list of information. (Note: When you put two words together without an AND, most search tools use AND as the default.) It is often a good idea to use OR early in your searching when you want to look at a broad sample of what is available on your topic. *Use OR to broaden your search.*
- **Affirmative action AND diversity**—These search directions would provide you with all the sources that use both *affirmative action* and *diversity*. This would limit your search. You'd only get the information that happened to use both terms. If you want to focus on the implications of affirmative action on understanding racism and diversity issues, this would be a good choice.
- **Affirmative action AND class**—This strategy would provide you with only those sources about affirmative action that mention something about class issues. This is a good strategy to use when you have decided to limit your research to a narrowed aspect of you topic. *Use AND to narrow your search.*
- **Affirmative action NOT diversity**—Use NOT to eliminate false hits. Whether you would want to use NOT in this case depends on the direction your research is moving. In some cases, NOT can be quite helpful. If you want sources that relate to written composition, search for "composition NOT music" to eliminate references to composing musical scores.

Here are some additional suggestions for developing your list of keywords:

- **Use "truncation" of terms to expand a search.** Truncation refers to dropping letters on either side of the search term. Use right-side truncation to expand a search. For example, if you want to find information on both astrophysics and astronomy, you can search for "astro" and you'll retrieve results on all words that begin with those letters.
- **Develop a list of synonyms for your topic.** Then insert OR between your words so that you get as expansive a list of terms as possible. For example, search for "affirmative action OR race relations OR diversity OR . . ." As you begin getting results, you'll have a better sense of what synonyms to use.
- **Check the subject field of the online record for a book and/or article.** You will find other subject terms listed. You can do subject searches using these terms to help you find additional references.

■ **Examine the bibliographies of several sources.** After you identify several key sources, examine their bibliographies. Each field uses terms differently. Thus, if you use the same key words as are used in your sources, you'll have a better chance of finding information.

■ **Read several key articles on your topic, and note commonly used terminology.** To find out how terms are used in the field of study you are exploring, read several articles on your topic and note what terms are used most frequently. Getting to know the language of your sources will help you locate appropriate information.

■ **Write down the most important words related to your topic or subtopic.** Keep your list handy so that you can add to it as you locate additional terms.

PRACTICE BOX

1. Keep a log of what you do and discover as you go through a search. For example, start by indicating what search engine you use, such as WebCrawler, Lycos, or Alta Vista. Use the broader categories of the search engine as you begin searching. What topics or hits does the search engine provide you with? Now do the same search using another search engine. How do the two searches differ? That is, what different hits does each search turn up even though you begin with the same original search topic? Share your results and experiences with others to develop your own suggestions on which search engines to use and how to use each most effectively.

2. Compare the bound volumes of *Library of Congress Subject Headings* in your library with the online Library of Congress site: http://lcweb.loc.gov/. Which is easier for you to use?

3. Experiment using Boolean search techniques with the words AND, OR, and NOT. How did using Boolean search techniques help your search?

Develop a System for Note Taking and Organizing Sources

When you begin to find valuable sources, you are ready to start taking notes. Develop a method for recording and organizing your notes, keeping track of your sources as you go.

Some researchers use a version of the popular note-card technique—using one set of three-by-five-inch cards for notes and a separate set of cards for bibliographic information about the sources from which the notes are taken.

Other researchers prefer keeping a research notebook in which they record the date they accessed a given item and the notes they want to have for later retrieval. Whatever your preferences, consider developing electronic equivalents, especially because of the ease with which you can download portions of texts for later use, capture lists of bibliographic data to disk, or copy and paste the location of Web sources into a separate file without making errors by retyping them. If you take time to gather snippets of information that you have downloaded, you should consider organizing that information into an electronic set of note cards. You can either put all your notes into one file, or create a separate file for each note.

Prepare a Working Bibliography

Bibliographies are lists of books, journals, articles, recordings, Web sites, or other resources. Bibliographies sometimes cover just the literature of one academic field; other times, bibliographies cover subdisciplines or even individual authors. You can prepare a working bibliography by referring to available bibliographies on your topic or by creating your own list of sources.

Bibliographies improve the likelihood that your research will be productive. When you use a published list of resources, you are starting from a much stronger base then when you begin your search on your own; you have the results of someone else's legwork. Aided by a bibliography, you can survey a much broader list of resources in a shorter period of time.

See if your library or another library on the Internet has a specialized bibliography on your topic, known as a reference bibliography. Sample reference bibliographies are included online in many libraries. Check the Cornell Library, which includes bibliographies for both their current classes and according to broad subjects, prepared by faculty or librarians with an interest in the topics. For specific class bibliographies, go to:

http://www.library.cornell.edu/okuref/classbibs.html

For the broad subject guides, go to:

http://www.library.cornell.edu/okuref/subguides.html

If you search the Web for the topic of your choice, you can find bibliographies on almost any topic. Libraries offer collections of bibliographies and post them on the Web. Metronet <http://www.metronet.lib.mn.us/lc/lc5.html> lists many of the kinds of bibliographies you can find. Here are just a few:

History of Technology Bibliography, Stanford University
Martin Luther King Jr. Bibliography, Stanford University
Shakespeare's Plays and Sonnets, Dartmouth University
Sea Turtle Bibliography, Florida State University System
International Labour and Radical History, Memorial University of
    Newfoundland
Foreign Law, Library of Congress

In addition to exploring the Web, explore any CD-ROM database or online databases available to you. Finally, consult print bibliographies such as the following in your library:

- *Sheehy's Guide to Reference Sources* (1986)
- *The Humanities: A Selective Guide to Information Sources* (1988)
- *Social Sciences Reference Sources: A Practical Guide* (1990)
- *The Social Sciences: A Cross-Disciplinary Guide to Selected Resources* (1989)

Validate Your Sources

All your sources need to be evaluated or validated. You need to determine whether the content is accurate, whether the author is an expert on the topic, whether the treatment of the topic is fair or biased, and whether the information is current. Finally, you need to consider whether the information is appropriate for your needs.

Most of the time you want to locate the most scholarly, convincing sources on your topic—sources that will help you prove the claim you are making about your topic. Occasionally, you will *want* to use a biased source or a source that is not written by an expert. You may want to demonstrate the range of opinions that were held by people from both parties on the topic of impeaching President Clinton. If so, quotes from listservers and newsgroups, often considered unreliable sources, could be totally appropriate for your needs. What determines whether a source is useful in your paper is the purpose the source serves in your argument.

But even though it has always been important to validate sources, Internet sources are more troublesome to analyze than print sources. You may have difficulty locating the author, you may not be able to determine the source of publication, and as a result, you may not detect bias in your source. For example, if you locate information on archaeological resources, it might take you quite some time to determine that, since the author is a travel buff rather than a trained researcher, the commentary on his or her Web pages may not be reliable. (See Chapter 5 for a more thorough discussion of evaluating sources.)

Draft, Revise, and Edit Your Paper

Remember that a research paper should not just present the information, it should interpret it. Take time to go over your sources many times, thinking and reflecting about the issues and ideas they present. After you develop your own focus, start drafting. Present information from your perspective, being sure to use sources to support your points.

Use whatever writing process is most appropriate for you and for your topic. Some writers work best from outlines; others use jot lists, and still others plunge right in and begin drafting. If you have organized your information carefully, you should be able to access your notes as you write.

During the drafting process, keep in mind that you should refocus and adjust your topic as you go. When you have questions that your current set of notes doesn't answer, return to the Web or the library and look for sources that help. Or write to peers in your classes about issues and problems that emerge as you write and ask them to provide you with feedback.

The act of writing usually helps writers to get to know their topic better than they knew it before. Allow the drafting process to be an interactive one. As you write, interact with your sources, questioning them, challenging them. If you change your mind about your thesis as a result, so be it. Keep open the possibility of change. Expect to discover that you need more sources.

Reserve some time toward the end of your research and writing to do a thorough revision of your text. If possible, have another reader suggest possible changes.

Remember to document your sources as you write. Although you don't need to worry about citation format as you draft, you do need to make sure that you indicate the exact page reference or data in parentheses so that you will be able to locate the source later. You can revise for correct documentation style during a final proofreading and editing session. Chapter 8 focuses exclusively on citing and documenting sources.

CONCLUSION

There is no single research process that will be right for everyone, just as there is no single writing process that works for every writer. Different writers inevitably prefer different writing and searching strategies. So customize what

 PRACTICE BOX

If you have already developed expertise using the Web or Internet:

1. Send your group members or your teacher an e-mail message describing what you have decided to write about and indicating to what extent online searching may have influenced your selection of topics. Give at least one example to demonstrate your conclusion.

2. If you already know how to access the Web site for this book, try posting your message to the bulletin board area at the end of Chapter 1 <http://www.prenhall.com/rodrigues>.

3. If your local library is accessible from the Web, explore its holdings directly through its Web page. As you learn more about how to search your library's Web page, share hints with other students about ways to make your searching more efficient.

you do to suit your own needs, but do try to develop organized research habits. With the array of information available on the Web and in the library, you need to be especially careful to develop sensible, yet creative, research procedures.

Electronic research processes are still emerging. After trying out several of the techniques suggested in this chapter, you will be in a position to critique them and to develop more appropriate processes for conducting library and Web research. Share your insights into electronic research with your classmates. Together, you will have a fuller and deeper insight into the possibilities than you ever could have developed alone.

EXERCISES

1. Select a preliminary topic for your research project. After you have selected a topic, do some preliminary reading. Summarize the key issues that the readings address. If you try to narrow your topic before reading a variety of sources, you may start down an unproductive research path.

2. Based on the reading you have done and the issues you have summarized, brainstorm a list of research questions that you might pursue.

3. After you have identified your research questions, revisit your preliminary topic and develop a working thesis statement to guide you as you continue your research.

4. Decide which research methodologies you will use and include the following possibilities: library research, Web research, survey research, observation, and personal interviews.

5. *Optional*: Work with a group of students on a topic of common interest. If each of you selects a different aspect of the topic, you can share research with one another as you proceed. Often, you can use the same sources for many different points.

SUGGESTIONS FOR RESEARCH

1. Do a research project on the nature of research writing in the information age. Has the Web already changed the nature of research assignments? You could explore the syllabi for various courses in your major that have been posted to the Web at schools around the country. (Note: If you are fairly new to searching, you may want to wait until you have read Chapter 2 before undertaking this research project.)

2. How do students and/or professionals *really* conduct research? See if you can determine whether some people actually follow steps in the research process in the way they are presented in books and on Web sites. Or see if

most people use these steps as a general framework but vary enormously in their own approach to research.

3. The Internet began as a place for scientists to exchange research results. Explore the continued nature of research collaboration on the Web. For example, you could research ways librarians are collaborating to develop shared digital resources. You could investigate the ways that faculty work together on grants and articles. You could examine "writer's sites" on the Web, places where authors invite review by interested readers.

4. How has the Internet enabled businesses to work together throughout the world? You could examine how industry is able to conduct business, share knowledge, and develop products even though their research, development, and production facilities may be located in different parts of the world.

2 CHAPTER

Researching Library and Web

After completing this chapter, you should be able to do the following:

■ Develop a list of subject terms and key words to use in your search.

■ Locate a book on your topic in the library using the online catalog.

■ Locate periodicals using appropriate print indexes or online databases.

■ Understand the difference between subject directories and search tools on the Web.

■ Explore subject directories on your topic and locate pathfinder sites—sites with resources on your specific topic.

■ Explore several search engines, and determine which is best for your topic.

Your research projects in college will require you to search both library and Web—an overwhelming combined set of information resources. The only way you will be able to make sense of all this information is to learn how to search for and locate the best possible sources on your topic.

Where should you begin? If you know that you will need to rely on the Web intensely for your topic (because it is about a current issue and thus not covered in books or scholarly journals), then you will probably shift to Web searching earlier in the research process than will students who are writing about topics that are less current. Nonetheless, you need to learn the basics of using your library at the outset of your research process.

You are probably more familiar with the library than you are with the Web, so in this chapter we will first present some strategies you can use in conducting library research. Then we will turn to Web searching, introduce (or review for those of you with experience) some basic navigation techniques, and present some advanced search strategies. You should realize that you will have more difficulty validating the results of Web searching, but if you are willing to take the extra time and effort involved, you will reap the results.

WHAT IS THE LIBRARY? WHAT IS THE WEB?

The distinction between the Web and the library is becoming harder and harder to make. The "free" portion of the World Wide Web—including many traditional library resources, such as newspapers and some journals—is available to anyone. The subscription portion of the Web, however, is only available to those who have subscribed. Subscription to online periodical indexes (which will be explained in this chapter) are often available only to patrons— in the case of public libraries, to those individuals who have library cards and, in the case of institutional libraries at colleges and universities, to faculty, staff, and registered students.

Why this limited access to some resources? Most books, magazines, and journal articles are still under copyright protection. The authors and publishing companies who develop these materials do so for profit; thus, use of the resources is limited to those who have paid to use them—either institutions and their clientele or individuals who purchase private subscriptions to the increasing number of online databases that are available by individual or institutional subscriptions.

Similarly, the distinction between the physical library and virtual extensions to physical libraries are sometimes confusing to students. Your institution's library is more than the sum of all the books, print journals, newspapers, etc., that you can see and touch in the physical building called a library. Your institution's library includes whatever online resources it has purchased and made available through a login point on its library Web page.

Let's look at the authors' library as an example (see Figure 2.1). The University of Texas at Brownsville library (http://academics.utb.edu/library/) has a limited collection size, since it has a limited library budget. But the virtual library has an impressive collection of encyclopedias, indexes, and journals.

If you search for "affirmative action" in the library catalog, you will not find books from the current year. But if you search the online databases, you have an enormous range of selections. Of course, the World Wide Web extends the possibilities still further, since you can locate headline news on late-breaking events related to the topic at many Web sites. Also, you can access government resources to learn more about your topic. No longer do students at institutions with limited resources have to feel cheated because they do not have the same size physical library. And with interlibrary loan, they can access books and articles at most any library in the world.

Try to locate all types of sources—Web sources, books, and journal articles in online databases, as well as any appropriate print journals. Relying too heavily on one type of resource (whether a library or a Web source) can limit your perspective.

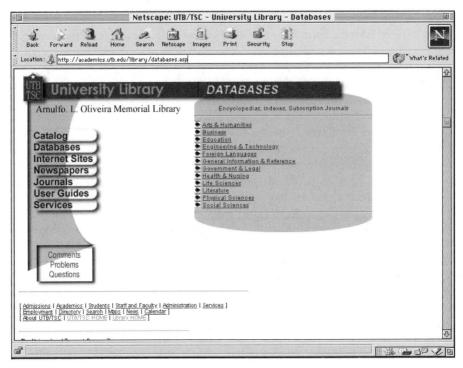

FIGURE 2.1 Home page for library at the University of Texas at Brownsville.

EXPLORING YOUR LIBRARY

When most people think about searching for information, they probably think first of books and magazines. These resources are still available in the physical library, but some of them have already begun to migrate to the Web. Take time to learn which resources are available to you, in what locations, and in what format. You'll need this information not only for your current research project but for your continuing research tasks, both in college and at work.

The Physical Library

Begin by looking for a reference desk near the reference collection. This is a likely place for you to find specialists called reference librarians whose job it is to help you locate the information you need. If you ask for help on your research project, most librarians will ask if you have already checked the reference collection for background information on your topic.

Reference sources include the following kinds of books: dictionaries, encyclopedias, handbooks on specialized topics, news digests, yearbooks (annual events on specific topics), almanacs, atlases, bibliographies, government publications, and—perhaps the most important reference resources—indexes and abstracts of periodicals.

Make sure that you locate the print indexes and abstracts, large sets of books that index articles from different types of periodicals. Print indexes, such as *The Reader's Guide to Periodicals Index* and *The Social Sciences and Humanities Index* may also be available in a digital version in your library's collection of online databases (see Indexes and Databases discussed later).

Explore other areas of your local library including the following places:

- **Periodicals Section**—Periodicals include newspapers, scholarly journals, and magazines. Find the bound periodicals—periodicals that have been stitched or glued together and shelved according to title—and the unbound periodicals—new magazines, newspapers, and scholarly journals that you can read in the library.
- **Microfiche Collection**—Area in the periodicals section of the library that keeps a collection of periodicals on special film called "microfiche." To read articles in these journals, you need to use a microfiche reader.
- **Interlibrary Loan Office**—Office or desk where you can fill out forms indicating which journal or book you would like to order from another library in the country. Sometimes there is a small charge for this service.

Knowing the location of items in your library will allow you to return to them as needed during your research process. Many materials in the print collection of your library will be useful to you in your research. For example, material in your library's reference area can provide important background information on your topic. Check to see what is available so that, after you have explored online databases, you know what else you have to choose from. Don't overlook the obvious. Journals and newspapers that your library subscribes to in hard copy (print) are often the most valuable sources you can locate.

The Card Catalog

Many libraries have moved their online catalogs to the Web. If that is the case in your library, then to locate books, you need to know how to use a Web browser to search your library's card catalog, the collection of library holdings that can be searched by subject, title, or key word. In some libraries, you may still need to use a card catalog that consists of drawers of index cards—some categorized by author, some by title, and some by subject. Some libraries that have online card catalogs maintain their print card catalog, if not for current holdings, then for resources that were acquired before the library went online.

As books are purchased, librarians catalog them. The cataloging consists of assigning a call number to each source using, in most cases, the Library of Congress system of classification, which uses an alphanumerical scheme to categorize books (see Figure 2.2). Some small libraries and many public libraries, however, still rely on the older Dewey Decimal System of classification, which sorted books using a numeric scheme.

How should you begin to search for books or other print resources? In most cases, you should begin by using subject headings to search the online card catalog. You probably did not realize it, but the subjects into which librarians sort your sources are based on official categories that librarians have agreed to nationally. The four-volume set of the *Library of Congress Subject Headings* (typically located in the reference area of your library) contains the official list of subject headings agreed on by librarians. If you look up a term using the *Library of Congress Subject Headings*, you will be presented with a range of optional terms that you can use to search for your topic. For example, looking up "presidents" will lead you to alternative subject headings that might be useful for you to use: "heads of state" is the broader term (BT is the abbreviation used); narrower terms (NT) suggested include "children of presidents," "grandchildren of presidents," and "women presidents." Related terms (RT) include "ex-presidents" and "executive power."

Many libraries list their periodicals in the library catalog. If yours does, you are lucky, for then you can find out if your library has a given periodical and, if so, where that periodical is located—on the shelves or in an online database. Go to the periodicals area in your library and learn where the current periodicals as well as the bound serials are located.

A — General Works
B — Philosophy, Psychology, Religion
C — Auxiliary Sciences of History
D — History: General & Outside the Americas
E — History: United States
F — History: United States Local and America
G — Geography, Anthropology, Recreation
H — Social Sciences
J — Political Science
K — Law
L — Education
M — Music
N — Fine Arts
P — Language and Literature
Q — Science
R — Medicine
S — Agriculture
T — Technology
U — Military Science
V — Naval Science
Z — Library Science and Information Resources

FIGURE 2.2 Library of Congress classification.

PRACTICE BOX

1. Find the card catalog in your library. If it is a computer catalog, search for a book on your topic. Print out the "record"—the information available about the book, including title, author, date of publication, and call number. Then locate the book and check it out. Jot down any problems you had in this process so that you can compare your experience with other students in your classes.
2. While you are in the stacks (area where books are shelved), take time to browse. Look at the books that are stored near the book you have selected. Jot down the names and call numbers of two or three books that you might want to explore later.
3. Find the reference section of your library. After you determine how the reference collection is organized, locate one book in the general subject area of your topic. For example, if you are exploring environmental pollution, you might find a reference book on health that will include a discussion of illnesses related to the environment. Jot down some notes about the possible value of this book to your research project.

Indexes and Databases

Most libraries now have online indexes, and most of these libraries have stopped purchasing the print equivalent of the index. As print indexes of periodicals migrate to the Web, they are often referred to as online or subscription databases.

What is a database? A database is an organized collection of information. A collection of online databases—searchable collections of journal titles, abstracts, and some full-text articles—are available in most libraries. Online databases tend to be specialized: a journal database is an organized collection of journal articles; similarly, a newspaper database consists of an organized collection of newspaper articles. A full-text database contains electronic versions of the original texts, such as judicial decisions, newsletters, or reference works. Once you learn how to use these databases, you will find them much easier to work with than print indexes.

Different kinds of databases are available, some specific to a given company, and others, specific to a given topic or publication type. That is, you can use a database such as "Poem Finder" to locate just one type of data—poems. Or, you can use newspaper databases to locate only newspaper articles. Find out what online databases are available to you in your library. See if you have databases that cover the topic of your research project or your major field of study. For instance, FirstSearch is a collection of databases that covers journal articles in science, technology, business, the humanities, and the social sciences. If you are a business major, you will want to learn how to use LEXIS-NEXIS and ABI Inform. If you are an English major, you don't want to overlook the Modern Language Association's online index.

Some databases are available in three formats: in print, on CD-ROM, and on the Web. Others are only available online. And some are still only available in print. Your library may provide only abstracts online, or it may have chosen to subscribe to commercial databases such as Wilson Select or ProQuest, which include the full text of articles.

Before using a database, take time to learn a little bit about how the data in each service is organized. If possible, locate a tutorial or guide on using that database. If your own library does not have a tutorial available, you may find one at another library site on the Web. Tutorials are available at sites such as the following:

Emporia Library
http://webbase.emporia.edu/slim/li812/project/812971/topic4c.htm
Here you will find a tutorial for searching Dialog.

Greenley Library of SUNY Farmingdale
http://www.farmingdale.edu/CampusPages/ComputingAndLibrary/Library/guides.html
Tutorials for searching LEXIS-NEXIS, ProQuest, and Searchbank are available here.

Each library decides what databases it will subscribe to, so this book cannot provide you with specific guidance in searching your databases, since there are so many available.

PRACTICE BOX

Learn as much as you can about the journal indexes and databases in your library. Answer the following questions:

1. Where are the online databases located in your library? (On the Web? On CD-ROM?)
2. Locate three databases that are likely to have resources on your topic or in your field of study.
3. Search for information on a key word (or set of words) related to your topic in all three databases. Which one gave you the most results? The best results?
4. Does your library have directions for searching these databases available to patrons? Where are they located?
5. If your library does not have directions for the database you need, locate directions that have been posted on the Web at another library. Which library did you find? What search engines and search terms did you use to locate that information?

EXPLORING THE WEB

People use the Web for different purposes. The strategies for basic navigation and searching are not much different for personal searching than they are for academic searching; however, if you will be using the Web for research, you will need to understand more than the general searcher needs to know. You should learn how to distinguish between search engines on the basis of which engine is best for locating which types of resources. Also, you should understand the differences between search engines and subject directories so that you can determine which will work better at different phases of your research process. This section will help you learn both the basic and the more advanced search skills that you will need. If you are a beginner, you can skip the advanced search section for now and return to this chapter when you have developed your skills.

NAVIGATING AND BASIC SEARCHING

Four strategies for navigating the Web are described in this section: Using the navigation panel of a Web browser, entering the URL into the location panel, using search tools and search strategies, and using bookmarks.

Using the Navigation Panel

From the startup home page you can move to many locations, depending on the hypertext links that have been incorporated into the page you are using. Sometimes links are underlined text areas; other times, such as on Prentice Hall's home page <http://www.prenhall.com>, they are simply text items that look no different from other text on the page until the cursor turns into a hand when it moves over them. You merely point and click with a mouse to move from the current location to the location that the Web designer has designated.

You can use the navigation panel (as shown in Figure 2.3) on your browser to move **Back** to each previous location you have visited. If you click on **Home**, you will return to the startup page. You use the buttons and other items on the navigation panel in conjunction with hypertext links to move from page to page.

Before attempting to collect information for your research paper, get comfortable browsing the Web. Learn how to do the following: use the hypertext links to jump to another page or to a totally new site; move to a previous page using the **Back** button; move forward a page at a time using the **Forward** button; use the **Go** button (sometimes called the **History** button) to view all the sites you have just visited.

Using the Location Bar to Enter URLs

The location bar of the Web browser is the area that shows the Web address, or Universal Resource Locator (URL), that you are currently viewing. In the sample Web page in Figure 2.3 the location bar shows the address for the Colorado

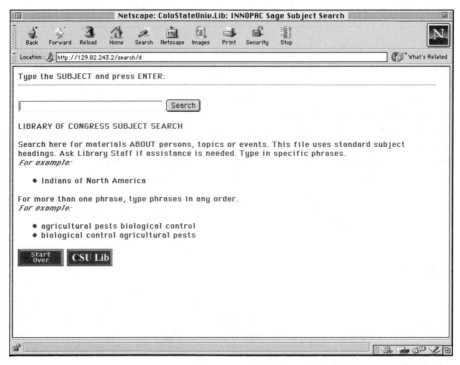

FIGURE 2.3 Netscape Navigator with navigation bar and location bar.

State University Library. To change to a new location (one that you have jotted down while listening to a television program, for example), all you need to do is delete the current address and enter a new one. To do this, move the cursor to the location bar and click on it. Then, delete the current address. Finally, enter the *exact* letters and numbers of the new address. Don't forget the slash marks! If you get an error message, it may be because the address you have typed in is no longer available for one reason or another—a set of library resources developed by a librarian may have been moved to a different server, or if the librarian has taken a new position, he or she may have moved the files too.

Using Search Tools and Search Strategies

Computer programs that help you retrieve information from all over the World Wide Web are called search engines. You are probably familiar with search tools if you have used a library's electronic catalog. Electronic catalogs use search engines to help you locate books by author, title, or key words. As discussed earlier, librarians use a standard set of terms from the Library of Congress called *Library of Congress Subject Headings*, thus making library searching somewhat easier than searching the Web. You can consult the subject headings (usually available in a book near the reference desk) to determine what terms will yield the best results.

Unlike the library, the Web has no common set of subject headings. Web publishers are not required to file their pages using preset terminology. Fortunately, Internet search engines have been developed to help Internet users locate information. By adopting efficient search strategies, you can become proficient in locating sufficient material on your topic.

Search Tools

There are two kinds of search tools: (1) search engines that search portions of Web databases and (2) subject directories—categorized, hierarchical sets of information that often include search engines as options.[1] With all search engines, you should develop effective search strategies, such as those described below.

Search engines.   A search engine is a program that tries to match key words that are entered into the search box with documents on the Web. Search engines use robot computer programs to scour the Web for sites and then return results to a main database. These robot programs are called "spiders" or "worms"; some work by searching only the opening paragraph of a Web page, whereas others search the full text. Search engines work in different ways. A search engine takes the words or phrases you enter into the search box on the screen and then goes through its database attempting to find matches to your search terms.

The relative strength or weakness of a search engine depends on how good the search engine is at locating the information you need and presenting it in a useful way. The automated kinds of search tools—including Alta Vista, Excite, HotBot, Infoseek, Lycos, and Web Crawler—use computer programs to locate information. Computer robots rove the Internet continually to gather information about new sites and to report that information to the computer that initiated the search.

Alta Vista
http://www.altavista.com
Alta Vista is the most comprehensive search engine. Because of its power and speed, Alta Vista will provide what it considers the best matches first. You may have to return to the search area and refine your search if the results are too extensive. If you use upper and lower cases in your search, Alta Vista will search for the words as typed. If you are searching for a phrase, put the phrase in quotation marks. Alta Vista is also a good site for finding sources from Usenet newsgroups. Alta Vista's major flaw is that results often include duplicates and lower-level pages from the same site.

---

[1]To locate a collection of search tools in Netscape, press the Search option on your browser. Then scroll down the page to view the variety of search tools included.

Advanced Features: An advanced technique that narrows the search is the capability of telling the browser to search for additional terms in specific fields of the Web site. For example, if you want a specific title you can type *title:* followed by the actual title.

Excite
http://www.excite.com
Excite allows you to use "concept-based searching" that does not require exact keywords, special punctuation, or Boolean terms. A major value of Excite is that it clearly ranks the best possible sites following your search. By choosing Excite's "more like this" link, you can zero in on sites that more clearly match what you are looking for. You may use Boolean search terms and quotation marks to identify specific phrases. The summaries of the sites located are highlights of those sites. Excite is also a good search engine for Usenet newsgroups and news articles.

HotBot
http://www.hotbot.com
HotBot automatically inserts AND between words that you type in the search box. If you do not want that, HotBot's search procedure allows you to narrow your search initially by using the drop-down menus. To search for a phrase use "the exact phrase" from the drop-down menu. If you prefer to control your Boolean search, you can select "the Boolean expression" from the drop-down menu.

Advanced Features: By selecting the "modify" link, you can access a drop-down menu that allows further refinements of the search. You can also narrow the search by date, by location or domain, any by special sites that contain various media.

Infoseek
http://www.infoseek.com
Infoseek can search for keywords, phrases in quotation marks, and capitalized names, but it does not use Boolean search terms. One of the best characteristics of Infoseek is that you can refine or narrow a set of results by selecting "search within these results" at the bottom of the page. You can ask questions. Using the drop-down menu, you can search for newsgroups, news, and other areas. Unlike Excite, Infoseek does not allow searching the news by date. Like Alta Vista, Infoseek allows you to use the field search terms *url:*, *site:*, *title:*, and *link:*. These allow you to determine how many other sites have links to a particular site Infoseek has identified.

Advanced Features: You can approximate Boolean searching by filling in boxes in the advanced search area.

Lycos
http://www.lycos.com
Lycos offers a simple way to search the Web, but does not allow refining or narrowing the search very easily. You can search for keywords or for phrases in quotation marks. You can use "+" instead of the Boolean AND and "−" instead of the Boolean NOT. Lycos is known for listing the top Web sites for various topics, which may allow you to begin your searches quickly with strong results. It is also a good site for finding sites with special graphics or sounds.

Advanced Features: You can customize your searches with Lycos Pro search techniques by using the "special" menu.

Web Crawler
http://www.webcrawler.com
Web Crawler allows you to use keywords, quotation marks around phrases, and Boolean search terms. It is owned by America Online (AOL) and comfortable for AOL customers to use. The relevance of sites located is determined by the ratio of the key words to the total number of words in a document or site. A distinguishing feature of Web Crawler is that the default or built-in setting is to list the sites without summaries.

Subject directories. Subject directories are Web sites that invite readers to look for information by first exploring general categories such as, Arts and Leisure, News and Views, or Health. Subject directories are created by people, not by the computer or the Web-searching software (called "spiders"). Though the quantity of sites available is limited compared to the quantity turned up by search engines, they may be more reliable when they locate topics that you want. You can often locate specialized subject categories ranging from agriculture to space technology. Subject categories or subject directories are most useful at the beginning of the research process, when you need to explore broad categories to get a general sense of what your topic is about. Once you have determined your topic more specifically, a more productive search would be yielded by a search engine.

Yahoo!
http://www.yahoo.com
Yahoo! is the premier subject category search site on the Web. Yahoo! lists Web sites by various categories. The sites listed are those recommended by people, not those identified by a search engine. If you know the category of what you are searching for, you can begin with the categories offered by Yahoo! and narrow the search by selecting the categories within those categories. You can use keywords, phrases in quotation marks, and + or − symbols to narrow your search. Yahoo! does not accept Boolean terms, but does accept the field terms *t* for *title:* and *u* for *url:*. Yahoo! also searches Usenet newsgroups.

The World Wide Web Virtual Library
http://www.vlib.org/
The World Wide Web Virtual Library might best be thought of as a library of subjects. When you access the home page, you find a list of subjects. By clicking on any of the subjects, you can narrow your search within the total subjects that have been entered into the Virtual Library. This "library" is compiled by over 200 "maintainers," whose job it is to update the library on a regular basis. Searching this site is much like using an encyclopedia. You may not find exactly what you want, but if you need to learn more about your subject or narrow your subject before beginning to use search engines, this might be a good place to start.

Search Strategies

Even though you can get reasonably good results without much trouble, you will get better results if you develop efficient search strategies. Here is a list of tips for searching that are just as useful in the library or commercial database as on the Web:

1. Learn to use Boolean operators.
2. Think in synonyms or phrases. Jot down a list of key words that come to mind, then list synonyms for each word. If you want, you can also list some phrases or clauses, for phrases and clauses help you focus on the thesis or angle you are exploring, e.g., affirmative action:
   - Synonyms: equal opportunity, fair employment
   - Antonyms: discrimination, discrimination in hiring
   - Clauses: Is affirmative action fair? (Search for "affirmative action" and "fair")

     Is affirmative action discriminatory? (Search for "affirmative action" and "discrimination")
   - Who is against affirmative action? (Search for "affirmative action" and "against" or "anti")
3. Before you use a commercial database (such as First Search or Dialog), take time to familiarize yourself with the way the search engine works. Each commercial database uses different truncation rules, and each indexes terms in different ways. Locate directions for using these databases either within the program itself or at your library or at another library's Web page. If your library doesn't provide directions, find a library that does and bookmark that page!

Using Bookmarks

Bookmarks allow you to save your favorite sites to a list so that you can return to them easily. Rather than type in the entire Web address (URL) every time you want to return to a site, all you do is open your bookmark file and click on the site you want to visit. You can use bookmarks as a partial substitute for note cards. If you learn how to create folders for sets of bookmarks on a given topic, you can organize all the sources you locate for a given research project into one folder (with as many subfolders as you want). In addition to research bookmarks, consider using bookmark folders to collect useful personal reference information or information about hobbies. For a more thorough discussion of bookmarks, see Chapter 7.

The techniques for creating and organizing bookmarks varies from one browser to another. Use the help menu in your browser to find directions for creating bookmarks.

ADVANCED SEARCHING

There are three different kinds of search pages on the World Wide Web: standard, metasearch, and unified search interfaces. Standard search engines work independently; each is designed to search in slightly different ways. Metasearch engines are programs that search the other search engines, giving you a one-step solution to searching several search engines. Unified search interfaces are collections of search engines, assembled on one page—sometimes in categories—so that you can select the search engine you want without moving to a new Web page. Experiment with several search engines as well as a meta-page and an all-in-one page to see what search strategy you like best.

After you have become comfortable and acquired some speed at doing basic searches, you will begin to feel frustrated with the inordinate number of hits that search engines generate. Advanced search features of programs such as Alta Vista, Excite, and Infoseek allow you to limit your search using advanced search commands such as the Boolean operators AND, OR, NOT, +, –.

Standard Search Engines

Standard search engines have been developed by individual companies to compete with one another. Each search engine has slightly different features than the next, to give it a unique selling feature. For example, Alta Vista boasts that it searches more Web pages than any other search engine and, as a result, returns the most hits. Infoseek, on the other hand, searchers fewer Web sites, but features a unique way of clustering its hits so that those found at the same site are grouped together.

Metasearch Engines

Metasearch engines are combinations of the other search engines. When a user enters a search query into the metabox, it sends the query to several search engines that, in turn, perform the search and return the results, which are reported in one comprehensive list. Why use a metasearch engine? If you are looking for very obscure information, metasearch engines will save you time, for they let you know up front whether the information is readily available or not.

There are some problems with metasearch engines, however. First, they can be misleading. As you know from searching individual engines, often you have to change terms several times before you get good results, and often the same set of terms that results in good returns on one search engine will be less successful on another. Using one set of terms for all search engines does not allow you to do interactive refining, which, ultimately, is the most effective way of searching. Further, in most cases, metasearch engines do not allow you to take advantage of the advanced search features of the standard search engines. Before you use a metasearch engine, learn how to use individual search engines effectively.

How do metasearch engines work? Many understand Boolean operators (and shortcuts such as +,–, and other signs). Some will even translate the symbols to match the unique needs of different engines (e.g., Alta Vista and Info-Seek use + and –, but some search engines use the standard AND, OR, and NOT). Below is a list of metasearch engines. Explore them until you find one that you like. Then bookmark it for future reference.

Surfy
http://www.surfy.com
Uses up to forty search engines at once.

Savvy Search
http://www.savvy.com
Searches the results of other search engines and claims to report the same results that you would get if you searched each engine separately.

Cyber 411
http://www.cyber411.com
Uses sixteen search engines. Translates syntax and eliminates duplicates.

Dogpile
http://www.dogpile.com
Uses twenty-five search engines. Offers time limits. Translates search syntax to match search engine. Provides remote pop-up box. Lets you decide the order you want it to follow when moving from one search engine to another.

Metacrawler
http://www.metacrawler.com
Includes directories with categorized lists of Internet information, such as travel and shopping sites on the Web. Accesses nine search engines. Lets users customize search queries for different engines. Searches both the Web and newsgroups, if you want. Lets users set limits on the number of results reported. Gives a relevancy ranking for returns—based on an average of the relevancy in the different search engines.

Unified Search Interfaces

Unified search interfaces assemble a range of engines on one page. You enter the queries into each and you get the results sequentially. Three examples of unified search interfaces are given below:

The All-in-One Search Page
http://www.albany.net/allinone
Provides 120 categorized engines (e.g., for Web page designers or for educators). Allows for different kinds of searching (e.g., home pages or e-mail addresses).

Beaucoup
http://www.beaucoup.com
Has 1,200 search utilities organized into categories. The Beaucoup search page is pictured in Figure 2.4. It focuses on subject searches, such as environmental concerns.

ISleuth
http://www.isleuth.com
Has three thousand search utilities covering a range of topics. After you type in a term, the program tells you which engines and directories would be best for finding answers. Specific subject categories lead you to special ISleuth pages that contain many subject databases which can be searched without leaving ISleuth.

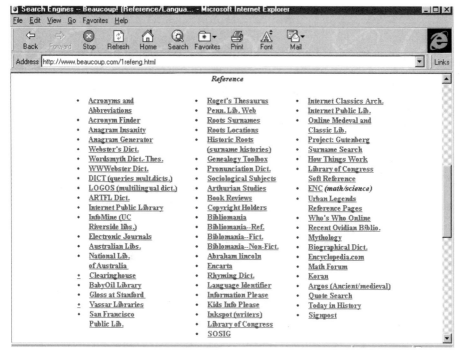

FIGURE 2.4   Beaucoup search page.

CONCLUSION

One thing you can count on with the Web and online catalogs is change. By the time you read this book, search engines will have changed as will some of the search strategies you need to use to locate information. But if you learn the basic principles of searching and become familiar with the kinds of search tools available on the Web and in library catalogs, you will be prepared to learn the new approaches that emerge.

Instead of thinking of the library or the Web separately, try to think of both together. For some topics, you will probably start searching on the Web. For other topics, you will begin with the library. Think of library databases and the library catalog as ways to extend your Web search. Similarly, think of the Web as a way to bring your library search up to date. In many cases, you will need to shuttle back and forth from library to Web many times.

EXERCISES

1. Using the topic you identified in Chapter 1, develop a list of potential key words and synonyms that will help you conduct your research.

2. Using these key words (and combinations of key words) develop a list of sources that you locate in your library (including your library's resources on the Web and print databases). As you are searching, continue to refine and revise your search terms.

3. Work with a group of students to learn how to use various databases available to you in your library. Assign a different database to each student in your group, who should become an expert on using that particular database. Then, at a time when you can all get together, teach each other how to use the different databases.

4. Use three different search engines to locate a parallel set of resources on the Web. Use the form below to guide you as you organize your results.

Key Words	Engine #1	Engine #2	Engine #3	Engine #4

5. Do a preliminary evaluation of your sources, using the following criteria for evaluating sources:
   a. Is this an authoritative source?
   b. Does it cover the topic sufficiently to be of use in your paper?
   c. Is the content current?
   d. Is the bias detectable?

6. Working in groups, share your research results. Help one another decide who needs to refine his or her topic further.

7. Now make a list of research questions that you want to pursue as you work your way through the next chapter.

3

Library Resources on the Web

After completing this chapter, you should be able to do the following:

- Locate and explore libraries on the Web.
- Determine which libraries have resources useful to you.
- Identify resources that will be useful for future projects.
- Locate and explore Web resources.

If you have access to the World Wide Web as you work on your research project, you need to explore both free, publicly available Web resources along with whatever library resources available at your institution or other colleges or universities, both in the physical library and online. Some of the library resources are traditional print resources; others are online databases of newspaper articles, magazines, and journals.

This chapter will help you locate libraries across the world. It also will help you understand what is available to everyone through the World Wide Web and through private subscription—either institutional or individual—to supplement your library resources.

FINDING LIBRARIES ON THE WEB

The Internet makes it possible for you to access not only your own library's catalog, but also catalogs from libraries around the world. Why would you want to search other libraries? In some cases, you may need to locate essential sources on your topic that your library does not have. In other cases, you may want to read titles and abstracts just to get a sense of what has been published on your topic. Searching in several catalogs can help you limit your topic and determine your research strategies.

You can locate almost any college library quite easily with just a standard Web search tool. Here's how you would proceed if you are using Infoseek, one of the search tools described in Chapter 2:

■ Click on **Search** on the navigation panel of your browser (either Netscape Navigator or Windows Explorer)
■ Click on Infoseek
■ Enter the name of the library of your choice in the search box (e.g., University of Texas at Brownsville Library)

When you locate the library's home page, find a link to the online catalog, and check to see if the library provides any directions for searching. Bookmark your library so you can return to it easily. (See Chapter 7 for information on bookmarking.)

Using a Library Access Site to Find Your Library

If your research requires you to use different online library catalogs, you should learn how to access libraries around the world in efficient ways. A useful way of finding the library of your choice is to use one of the many sites that have sprung up on the Web where librarians have made available either lists of other libraries or software that enables you to find any library in the world. To use these access lists, you need either to know the URL and type it into the location window of your browser or to use a search tool to locate the resources. Here's a list of particularly good resources. When you find them, be sure to bookmark them for ease of use.

Library Catalogs on the World Wide Web
http://www.lights.com/webcats/
A gateway to online catalogs across the World, libraries in this collection are listed by country and within the United States by state. To find the library of your choice, just select the state, then scroll down through the alphabetical list of institutions, and click on the library you are interested in exploring.

Library Servers on the World Wide Web
http://sunsite.berkeley.edu/Libweb/
The Berkeley Digital Library Sunsite, sponsored by the Library, University of California–Berkeley, and Sun Microsystems (see Figure 3.1). This site allows you to link to over seven hundred libraries across the world. It is kept up to date by librarians at the University of California–Berkeley.

Hytelnet on the World Wide Web
http://www.lights.com/hytelnet/
This site allows you to connect directly to Telnet sites without first downloading the software on your own machine. You can locate library catalogs that have Telnet

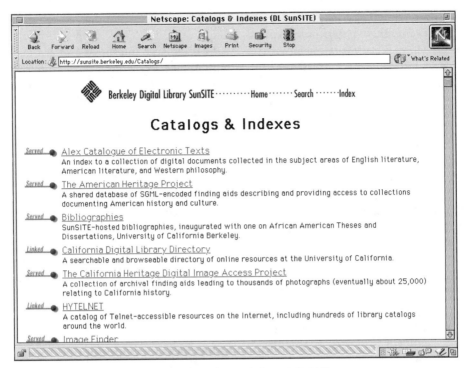

FIGURE 3.1   Catalogs and indexes in the Berkeley Digital Library.

access, as long as your computer has Telnet software loaded into it. You can even search by type of library, including medical libraries, law libraries, K–12 libraries, and public libraries. Some of the catalogs accessible by Telnet also have World Wide Web interfaces. One of the main reasons for continuing to provide Telnet access is to allow people who do not have powerful computers to access the libraries through text-only interfaces.

The Library of Congress Web Site
http://lcweb.loc.gov
The Library of Congress is taking an active role in Internet and Web development. Its collection includes links to the Library of Congress's book collection along with links to special collections, such as the American Memory Project.

EXPLORING LIBRARY CATALOGS

After you've located the library you want to use, then what? You may need to locate books, periodical indexes and databases, newspaper indexes, or online indexes and print indexes in these libraries. This section will help you with all of these. It will also help you decide how to determine what indexes—whether print or online—you should explore.

Many library catalogs now have World Wide Web interfaces and are easy to search. Others—in particular those with Telnet access only—are quite different from others. You will need to use different commands in different library catalogs to search for subjects, titles, and authors. If, for example, you've learned how to use the MELVYL system (in California), you'll discover that you cannot use those same commands when you use Harvard's HOLLIS system.

To solve the interface problem—the problem of having to learn many different ways of searching—librarians have been working on a standard method of catalog design. They have organized their catalogs in a way that enables the entire collection to be included in a Wide Area Information System (WAIS) database using what is called the Z39.50 protocol. WAIS is a program for searching specific collections of information that have been developed and stored on a special computer.

Figure 3.2 shows an opening screen for Z39.50 access. This Web site <http://lcweb.loc.gov/z3950/gateway.html> provides access to the Library of Congress collection along with other points, including the following:

United States Naval Academy, Annapolis (INNOPAC)
University of Arkansas, Little Rock (DRA)
University of Iowa (NOTIS)

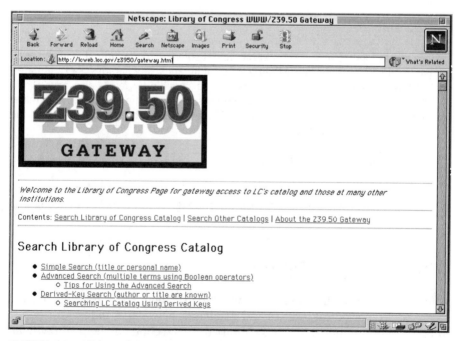

FIGURE 3.2 Library of Congress Z39.50 Gateway.

The Z39.50 standard searches use the form shown in Figure 3.3. You use this same form when you switch from one library that offers Z39.50 searching to another. Whenever you are developing a comprehensive bibliography on a topic, you should take time to locate sources in several libraries; at times like that, you'll realize the advantage that Z39.50 searching offers.

If you locate a book you want in another library, you will probably need to process an interlibrary loan request in order to get the book. Check to see if your library has an online interlibrary loan form. Also, find out if you must pay a fee for the interlibrary loan services.

TRADITIONAL LIBRARY RESOURCES ON THE WEB

You don't necessarily have to use a library catalog on the Web to locate resources traditionally found in libraries. Many standard resources are available on the Web—some on librarians' pages, others on a variety of pages produced by individuals and companies across the world. As you work on your research project, explore Web resources such as book pages, journals and magazines, online journals and zines, indexes and abstracts, and encyclopedias and other references.

Books on the Web

Many out-of-copyright books are available on the Web. These collections are massive, including all of Shakespeare's works, the Bible, poetry throughout

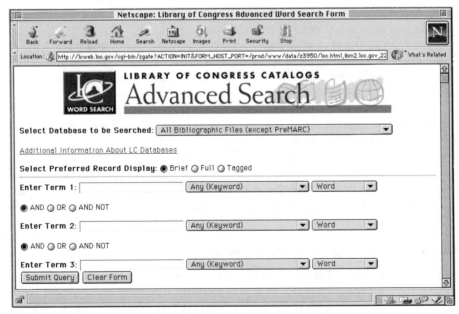

FIGURE 3.3 Library of Congress Catalogs Advanced Search.

the ages, and more. Two of the best sites for books are Project Gutenberg <http://promo.net/pg/> and Project Bartleby <http://www.cc.columbia.edu/acis/bartleby/>. Another online books page of note is:

The Online Books Page
http://www.cs.cmu.edu/books.html

This site includes sources in all disciplines, not just literature. For example, here is a partial list of books in the category "economics, trade, and transportation" included in the database:

- *A History of Political Economy* by John Kells Ingram
- *The Mercantile System and Its Historical Significance* by Gustav Schmoller
- *An Inquiry into the Nature and Causes of the Wealth of Nations* by Adam Smith
- *The Poverty of Philosophy* by Karl Marx, with contributions by Friedrich Engels (HTML at marx.org)

Along with books in the public domain, you will find a scattering of recent print publications. Some publishers make selected chapters of new books available on the Web as an advertisement, and other companies are making out-of-print copies of books available free (e.g., BiblioBytes at http://www.bb.com/index.cfm). But because books are typically written for profit, publishers and authors are not about to give them away freely.

You can, however, locate information about books on the Web, and you can even order them through the many online stores, such as Amazon.com, a virtual bookstore that has no physical counterpart <http://www.amazon.com> and Barnes and Noble <http://www.barnesandnoble.com/>, the online version of the popular bookstore chain. Barnes and Noble's site also allows you to search for out-of-print books.

You can access almost all publishing companies through the Web. A list of publishers is available at ACQ Webs Directory of Publishers and Vendors <http://www.library.vanderbilt.edu/law/acqs/pubr.html>. Some publishers specialize in online books.

One noteworthy online book project is the National Academy Press (NAP) <http://www.nap.edu/> an organization created by the National Academy of Sciences to publish the reports issued by the National Academy of Sciences, the National Academy of Medicine, and the National Research Council. At the NAP On-line Book Store, you can order books online, search for titles, or browse through the catalog. As with most online book stores, you can also shop for books using a virtual shopping basket.

Journals and Magazines on the Web

It may be some time before most of the magazines and journals you need to access for your research make their way to the free portion of the World Wide Web. Why? Even though it would be less expensive for journals to publish online instead of in print, Web publication is still not seen as similarly prestigious in most academic circles. And even though electronic journals can be distributed internationally in an instant, many researchers are reluctant to publish their work in these journals.

A good place to find a comprehensive list of journals and magazines on the Web is the ACQ Web's <http://www.library.vanderbilt.edu/law/acqs/journals.html> (see Figure 3.4).

Many sites contain collections of journals or magazines available on the Web. Here are some you can use as starting points:

CIC Electronic Journals Collection
http://ejournals.cic.net/index.html
An authoritative source of electronic research and academic serial publications.

Internet Consortium for Alternative Academic Publication
http://www.icaap.org/
An alternative to the traditional way of publishing journals, this organization hosts journals that are free of charge.

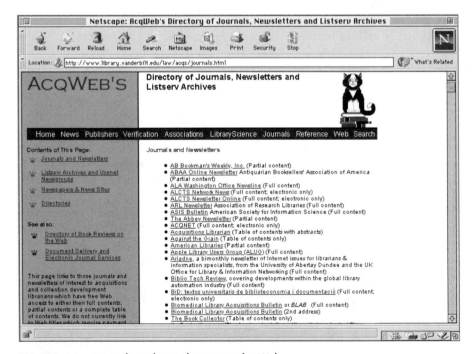

FIGURE 3.4 Journals and newsletters on the Web.

Academic Journals and Publishers
http://info.lib.uh.edu/wj/webjour.htm
Mostly scientific publishers are included on this list.

Index Morganagus
http://sunsite.berkeley.edu/~emorgan/morganagus/index.html
Full-text index of library-related electronic serials. Articles in more than eighty online titles including American Libraries Online, Australian Library Journal, Computers in Libraries, Current Cites, and TER (Telecommunications Electronic Review).

Directory of Electronic Journals and Newsletters
http://www.arl.org/scomm/edir/
Provides links to almost seventeen hundred electronic serials.

American Journalism Review Site
http://ajr.newslink.org/
Popular magazines indexed at this site include the following categories: Popular magazines; News and opinion; Business and professional; Computing; Lifestyle, people, and activities; and Magazine publishers.

Online Journals and Zines

Some magazines have developed online equivalents of their print journals. These magazines often add features that are not possible in print: *Atlantic Monthly Online* <http://www.theatlantic.com/index-js.htm> includes a forum area called "Post and Riposte" where readers can discuss recent articles; *Online U.S. News* <http://www.usnews.com/usnews/home.htm> has a forum too along with other interactive features, such as Citizen's Toolbox, that invite audience response.

Still another category is the zine—or Web magazine. What is a zine? How does it differ from a virtual journal or magazine? In some sense, all Web magazines could be called zines. But researchers should distinguish between magazines that are put out on a regular basis by an organized group, responsible to a specific constituency, and a zine put out by an individual or a private group. Although the individual or private group may be just as responsible and may have equal quality, anyone can publish on the Web. It is important to recognize that academic journals and regularly published Web magazines, which have to satisfy more people, usually have more quality checks than are necessarily present in publications by individuals. For a list of zines, see <http://www.zinebook.com>. Evaluation of all sources is critical (see Chapter 5).

Indexes and Abstracts on the Internet

You will find indexes and abstracts on the Web that are comparable to the ones available by subscription. Also, some—such as UnCover—can be searched, even if you do not subscribe. To get copies of the articles, you can pay (a steep price) or order them through interlibrary loan, or try to find a library that will provide you with access. (See if your public library subscribes to the database you want. If so, get a library card so that you will be allowed access to the online subscription indexes.) An online database you do not want to overlook is ERIC.

UnCover
http://www.wmich.edu/library/uncover.html
UnCover is an online database to which some institutions subscribe. UnCover provides access to the tables of contents for over 16,000 journals in various disciplines. Unlike most subscription databases, UnCover allows anyone to search its contents without charge. You can order articles directly from UnCover for about $10.00 each. If you locate an article you want to read, you should first check to see if your own library subscribes to that periodical. If not, you may be able to order it through interlibrary loan. For directions on how to search UnCover, check the guidelines developed by librarians at Western Michigan University.

ERIC
http://ericae.net/search.htm
ERIC is an educational database that consists of *Current Journals in Education* (CJIE) and *Resources in Education* (RIE). RIE is ERIC's bibliographic database of over 850,000 conference papers, reports, instructional materials, research articles, and other materials. CJIE is the journal article bibliographic database. CJIE indexes professional journals in education and related fields. RIE indexes unpublished documents and reports. These texts are available on microfiche in most libraries. The abstracts for these sources are accessible free of charge through the Internet.

Project Muse
http://muse.jhu.edu
You can search the database of Project Muse, a humanities database developed by Johns Hopkins University Press. Some journals in the database, such as *Postmodern Studies*, are available without a subscription.

Electric Library
http://www.elibrary.com
As with other online indexes, Electric Library allows you to search its contents. If you want to see the article itself, however, you need to pay a fee. Although most full-text services are only available if your school, public library, or place of employment subscribes to the service, Electric Library is available by subscription to individuals. (It offers a free thirty-day trial, but you need a valid credit card to use this service.)

Encyclopedias and Other References

Although many standard reference sources such as *Roget's Thesaurus* <http://www.thesaurus.com> and a hypertext version of *Webster's Dictionary* <http://www.m-w.com/netdict.htm> are available online, standard encyclopedias are still under copyright and thus are only available to libraries that subscribe to their services. If your college does not subscribe to any online encyclopedias, you may want to explore the possibility of getting an individual subscription.

Britannica <http://www.britannica.com/>, the Web site sponsored by the *Encyclopaedia Britannica,* is a database of Web sites that are classified, rated, and reviewed by Britannica editors. The site reviews are included in the results of a search. Because the editors use consistent criteria to rate sites, the results are all reliable. Encyclopaedia Britannica Online <http://www.eb.com/> is a subscription service. For approximately $5.00 per month, you can subscribe and have access to the complete listings in the print version of the encyclopedia.

The Internet community has developed some free encyclopedias to help keep information available to everyone, not just those who can afford to pay for it. The Free Internet Encyclopedia <http://clever.net/cam/encyclopedia. html/> is a wonderful example of the way people across the world have collaborated to build information resources that are needed, and it fills a gap that traditional encyclopedias don't cover, since its purpose is to provide access to information through the Internet. It is not, however, nearly as reliable as print analogs, since the entries have not been authenticated (checked for reliability by editorial boards or other responsible individuals).

To find standard references such as dictionaries and style guides on the Web, use a search tool such as Infoseek or Alta Vista and search for the type of tool you want—dictionary, encyclopedia, etc. When you find items that you want to refer to repeatedly, bookmark them. (See Chapter 7 for suggestions on how to organize your bookmarks.)

Librarians at many universities have assembled Web collections of references sites. Here are a few particularly valuable reference sites to explore:

The Internet Public Library's Ready Reference Collection
http://www.ipl.org/ref/RR/
Created by librarians from the University of Michigan, sample resources in this collection include items such as almanacs, associations and organizations, biographies, calculation tools, calendars, census data, dictionaries, encyclopedias, periodical directories, and telephone books.

The Virtual Reference Desk at University of North Carolina–Chapel Hill
http://metalab.unc.edu/reference/quickref.html
This collection includes general reference as well as subject-area collections.

The Virtual Reference Desk at Purdue University (THOR)
http://thorplus.lib.purdue.edu/reference/index.html
An excellent source, this collection includes topics such as phone books, maps, and zip codes.

Newspapers

Even though some newspapers offer only subscription access, most newspapers are available for no fee. Some newspapers, including the *New York Times,* require you to go through a registration process the first time you access their site. As you examine different newspapers, notice that some have incorporated new features to tap the potential of the Web. For example, the *New York Times* has an online forum that takes the print-based notion of letters to the editor to a new level of interactivity.

A newspaper site to explore as a possible resource for your research is the *American Journalism Review*'s News Link <http://ajr.newslink.org/news.html>. It includes links to newspapers and news services such as the Reuter's News Media, Newspaper Association of America Web Site, *Chicago Tribune*, *Christian Science Monitor*, *Los Angeles Times*, *New York Times*, *Wall Street Journal*, *Washington Post*, and (London) *Times*.

Government Publications

Government offices have moved to the Web quickly. Not only does being on the Web help the organization save on expenses, it also serves as a public relations tool. People are happier with an agency whose services and information they can access speedily. Some government sources you should explore are listed below. If you go to the Web site for this text <http://www.prenhall.com/rodrigues>, select this chapter and explore the Web links section. The items listed below are included there, and you can bookmark those that you want to keep in your personal bookmarks collection.

A word of caution: be sure that the page you access is an authentic government page. Since any person or business can create a home page, try to determine the producer of the information and use your judgment. A good indication that the site is produced by a division of the government is *.gov* or *.mil* (military) in the site's address. Also pay attention to the introduction or "about this site" information at the Web site.

Some excellent government sites include the following:

The Federal Web Locator
http://www.law.vill.edu/Fed-Agency/fedwebloc.html
The Federal Web Locator is a service provided by the Center for Information Law and Policy and is intended to be the one-stop shopping point for federal government information on the World Wide Web. You can search the Legislative branch, the Judicial branch, or the Executive branch. In addition, you can explore agency sites and the sites of federal boards and commissions.

The US Census Bureau
http://www.census.gov/
Provides source for social, demographic, and economic data.

Government Printing Office GPO Access
http://www.access.gpo.gov/su_docs/
GPO provides access to government information through full-text storage of critical federal documents, such as the Code of Federal Regulations, the Congressional

Record, etc. It also provides Pathway Services to find items grouped by keywords, topics, agencies, or titles, and a database of items for sale.

Thomas—Legislative Information on the Internet
http://thomas.loc.gov/
Provides current U.S. federal legislative information, bills, laws, Congressional Record reports, and links to further information.

PRACTICE BOX

1. Browse through the list of electronic journals. Locate three journals on either your topic or in your field. Write an e-mail note to your instructor in which you describe the usefulness of these journals to your topic.
2. Find at least two books on your topic in a library other than your own. Write a note indicating what you found and any difficulty you had in finding it.
3. Find one journal in the list of journals at the International Consortium for Alternative Academic Publication page: http://www.icaap.org/journals.html.

CONCLUSION

Even though the Web has much to offer, the resources available in your library and the online databases to which it subscribes have much more—in most cases. Aside from current topics, such as those that depend on legal information or government documents available on the Web, you need to devote a significant portion of your time to exploring library journals, subscription databases, and books. In the future, it may be possible for students to complete research projects online, but for some time, researchers will need to spend considerable time in the library itself.

EXERCISES

1. Explore your topic in several libraries. If you locate promising sources and if time permits, order books or periodicals not available in your library through interlibrary loan.
2. Examine several libraries and note the differences in the types of resources they provide to patrons on their Web pages.

3. Find the following types of resources and evaluate their potential value to you as you work on your current research project:

   ■ Databases that allow you to search for information but not retrieve it without paying a fee (UnCover, Electric Library, *Encyclopaedia Britannica*)

   ■ The Internet Encyclopedia

   ■ The Internet Public Library

CHAPTER

Finding Resources
in the Disciplines

After completing this chapter, you should be able to do the following:

■ Explore discipline-specific resources on the Web (for either current or future research projects).

■ Identify and learn how to use online databases in your subject area.

Different fields of study value different kinds of research. If you are conducting scientific research or doing a paper for the natural sciences, you will have different needs when you search for sources than someone in the social sciences or humanities. This chapter focuses on locating discipline-based information on the World Wide Web. Take time to learn what key resources in your field are available at your library first, then use the Web to complement your search.

FINDING RESOURCES IN YOUR FIELD

As you begin to do serious research in your discipline, you have much to learn that is beyond the scope of this book. You need to learn about the professional organizations in your field, the major books, the key reference sources, and the leading journals. Each kind of source serves a different purpose in your research. Armed with a general command of the sources respected by the professionals in your field, you will be ready to learn what the Web holds for you.

You need to determine the exact nature of resources in your discipline. Some of the most valuable resources to explore are available in databases accessible through the Web *only* by subscription. In most cases, subscriptions are available for institutions and not individuals. If your institution does not have the online database, it may have the print index and may subscribe to the journals in print format.

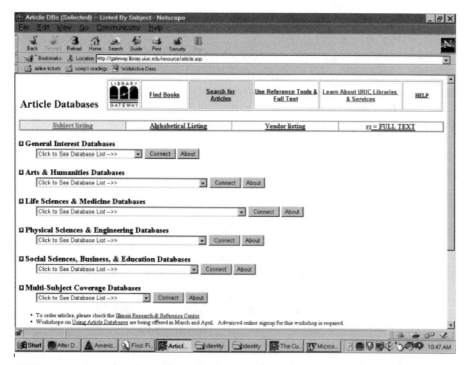

FIGURE 4.1 Results of search for databases in Sociology.

You may be able to find a list of resources in your discipline on your college or university library's Web site. If your own institution does not have databases listed by discipline (some list by major clusters such as Humanities, Social Sciences, etc.), you can explore other library's Web pages. One good place to search is the University of Illinois Urbana–Champaign Web site: <http://www.library.uiuc.edu/sitesearchg.htm>. The "Search the UIUC Library Web Site" page allows you to enter keywords into a search box. If you enter a field of study such as sociology, the result will include not only subscription databases, but Web sites related to this field. Figure 4.1 shows the results of this search. Notice the integration of library and Web sites on the same page.

For a good overview of databases available in different subject areas, try using the collection available from the Princeton Library <http://libweb.Princeton.EDU:2003/databases/web_subject_guides.html>. This collection includes subject guides to Web and library resources. Even if your library doesn't have the resource, you may be able to learn enough here to see if you want to track down an interesting source. For example, if you are looking for resources on African American History, you'll find an invaluable collection of resources, including the following:

■ Facts on Africa
■ African journals

■ Electronic news and listservs
■ Princeton's African Studies Department

Another good site for exploring databases in different fields is University of Tulsa's Index of Databases <http://www.lib.utulsa.edu/database/othrdb.htm>. You won't actually be able to access these, unless you are student at that university or unless your own library owns the database, but you can sort and search by discipline and develop a sense of what to look for in other libraries.

Always try to identify scholarly journals in your field, including nonsubscription sources available online that are respected by scholars in the discipline you are researching.

PRACTICE BOX

Whether your library has print, CD-ROM, or online journals, or some combination of all three, what you really need to know is which databases are available for your specific discipline. Using the list below as a starting point, check your library to see which journals are available for your subject area.

Business
ABI Inform
Business Periodicals Index
Education Index
Social Sciences Index

Book Reviews
Book Review Digest
Book Review Index
Choice
Reader's Guide to Periodical Literature

Language and Literature
Essay and General Literature Index
Education Index
Humanities Index
Social Sciences Index

History
Biography Index
Historical Abstracts
Humanities Index
Social Sciences Index

Religion and Philosophy
Essay and General Literature Index
Humanities Index
Index to Religious Periodical Literature

Literature
Art Index
Biography Index
Essay and General Literature Index
Education Index

USING SUBJECT-AREA COLLECTIONS AS STARTING POINTS

To locate resources in your discipline on the Web, gain a basic familiarity with key subject-area collections. Subject-area collections contain organized links about various topics or fields of study. These compendiums of information, in turn, contain pointers to specific subject-area data. Many subject-area collections have been gathered by people with interest and expertise in a particular field of study. Some collections, however, are merely random assortments of sites that have not been evaluated by a specialist or by a subject-area librarian. Use the criteria for evaluating Web sites in Chapter 5 when you decide which subject-area collections to use in your research.

Locating Subject-Area Collections

You can try two approaches. First, you can use your favorite search engine to locate subject-area collections in your discipline. For example, to find general subject-area collections, use a search engine, such as Alta Vista or Infoseek. Try using keywords such as the following terms: "subject-area collection" or "subject-area guide."

Your search will result in a list of sources on your topic. Examine these resources to see if any are useful to you. Next, refine your search. This time, locate only those items that pertain to your subject area or to your research topic. See Figure 4.2 for an example of a search for "subject-area guide engineering."

Review the most promising sites that you locate and jot them down in your research notebook. This list of sites may be helpful to you as you develop a bibliography for your research paper.

FIGURE 4.2   Results of search for subject-area guides.

Another approach you can use is to locate a page that collects subject category pages—a unified search page (see page 30) that focuses on subject searching, such as The All-In-One Search Page <http://www.albany.net/allinone>, which provides 120 categorized engines on specific topics, or Beaucoup <http://www.beaucoup.com>, which includes twelve hundred search utilities organized into categories.

Evaluating Subject-Area Collections

Subject-area collections that you locate with search engines are not necessarily good sources for your research. You need to take time to evaluate the sites you locate, just as you need to evaluate each individual source of information you use in your research. In addition to the general criteria for evaluating sources, consider these additional points when you evaluate subject-area collections:

■ How was the collection developed? By using a computer program to locate sites indiscriminately, or by having experts in the subject area develop or customize the site?
■ What is the audience for the site (e.g., the general public or specialists in the discipline)?
■ Does the collection include library and journal sources as well as Web sites?

PRACTICE BOX

Rank order the following list of subject-area collections from "most helpful" to "least helpful":
1. Lycos Community Guide—Humanities General
http://www-english.lycos.com/wguide/wire/wire_484527_49194_3_1.html
A guide developed for the Lycos search engine's home page
2. Accessing Our Humanities Collections
http://www.kcl.ac.uk/projects/srch/backgrd/guide/intro.htm
A guide to specialized collections for humanities researchers
3. The Zuzu's Petal Literary Resource
http://www.zuzu.com

GENERAL PURPOSE SUBJECT-AREA COLLECTIONS

Even though it is essential that you locate your own specialized subject-area collections, you should also know that several general purpose subject-area collections have developed considerable respect in the Internet community. Several of these—the World Wide Web Virtual Library, Argus Clearinghouse,

Einet Galaxy, BUBL link, and the Librarians Index to the Internet (Berkeley)— are described in this section. Additional subject-area collections are available at these sites:

Diane K. Kovacs' Internet Reference Collection
http://www.personal.kent.edu/~dkovacs/ref.html
Includes a link to the subject collection of scholarly e-conferences
<http://n2h2.com/KOVACS/Sindex.html>

Internet Subject Directories
http://www.albany.edu/library/internet/subject.html

INFOMINE: Scholarly Internet Resource Collections
http://lib-www.ucr.edu/

The World Wide Web Virtual Library

The World Wide Web Virtual Library <http://www.w3.org/hypertext/ DataSources/bySubject/Overview.html> is called a distributed subject catalog, since the contents of individual sections (discipline areas) are developed and kept up-to-date by contributors from different institutions. The list can be viewed in various ways: through an alphabetical list, category subtrees, or through a Library of Congress organizational structure. To find a collection of information on a topic of interest to you, select the overall cateogory, for instance "technology," then select appropriate subcategories. Eventually, you will locate individual sources. Take time to evaluate them and to add any valuable sources to your bookmark collection.

The Argus Clearinghouse

A selective collection of topical guides, the Argus Clearinghouse <http:// www.clearinghouse.net/> provides a way to access a set of guides that meet the standards set by the "Collection Development Policy," a set of criteria that determines whether or not a collection of resources will be added to the Argus Clearinghouse. One criterion, for example, is that a compiler must include his or her name and e-mail address as a way to help users determine the credibility of the submission. Submissions are reviewed by people, not by computer programs. Because this project is a nonprofit venture, the collection is not complete. To maintain standards, the reviewers follow a rating system which results in only 5 to 10 percent of all submissions being accepted. The rating system includes such criteria as level of resource evaluation, design of guide, organization of guide, and level of resource description.

Einet Galaxy

The Einet Galaxy <http://galaxy.einet.net/> is a list of sources dating back to the early Internet days. Originally a Gopher service called Gopher Jewels, developed by David Riggins of the University of Southern California, this site has been incorporated and is now referred to as the Einet Galaxy. Each subject area in the collection includes a fully searchable index. Here is a partial list of subjects you will find at Einet: government, humanities, law, leisure, medicine, reference, science, and social sciences.

BUBL (Bulletin Board for Libraries)

BUBL <http://bubl.ac.uk/link/> is aimed at the United Kingdom. Its introductory page includes help and links to subject areas. Information is carefully organized and cataloged. The catalog fields include title, author, subject, abstract, and class number. The "link" service is organized on the basis of subject categories in the Dewey Classification system. Browsing is much like looking at an assortment of books on a library shelf.

BUBL journals include the following subject areas: information science (LIS), computing and information technology (IT), medical services, business and marketing, and food sciences. Several magazines and newsletters as well as academic journals are included.

Librarians Index to the Internet (Berkeley)

The Librarians Index to the Internet <http://sunsite.berkeley.edu/InternetIndex/> is maintained by Carole Leita, a librarian at Berkeley. The site is supported in part by Federal Library Services and Technology Act funding and is administered by the California State Library. This is a comprehensive list of resources in many different subjects. Because it is a funded project, it is updated regularly.

A COLLECTION OF RESOURCES IN THE DISCIPLINES

Although you will need to locate sources for your discipline and for specific projects yourself, you may want to consider including some of the sites in this section, for they have each developed a reputation for excellence in their respective fields. A brief description of what constitutes research in each field of study and the style guide usually used by scholars in that field are included for the benefit of novice researchers.

Humanities

Humanities scholars focus on texts. What most college students think of as a research paper is really the humanities' version of a research project, using library research as the primary research technique. Humanities researchers develop their insights by reading and reviewing text-based research, such as analyses of literature, interpretations of history, and critiques of art. Humanities researchers typically use the Modern Language Association (MLA) Style

Guide (see Chapter 8). Often in humanities papers, you are asked to support your own opinion. Always do considerable background reading to help you develop a tentative research question that can guide you as you work your way through the sources you locate. Here is a list of some respected humanities sites:

Carnegie Mellon English Server
http://english-www.hss.cmu.edu

American Verse Project
http://www.hti.umich.edu/english/amverse/

Literary Resources on the Net
http://www.english.upenn.edu/~jlynch/Lit/

The Zuzu's Petal Literary Resource
http://www.zuzu.com

Electronic Text Center at the University of Virginia
http://etext.lib.virginia.eu/english.html

Center for Electronic Texts in the Humanities
http://www.princeton.edu/~mccarty/humanist/

Voice of the Shuttle
http://humanities.ucsb.edu/

H-Net (Humanities Online Home Page)
http://h-net.2.msu.edu/lists/lists.cgi

Social Sciences

Social scientists examine social issues. They recognize that the results of their work are relative, since they are dealing with people, not scientific data. Nonetheless, they value controlled investigation and use a variety of research techniques, including surveys, statistical analysis of data, interviews, focus groups, and participant observation studies (Zimmerman and Rodrigues). Some historians do humanities research; others do social research. The kind of research technique used determines whether the project is considered a humanities or a social sciences project. Oral history projects that rely on primary sources (recordings of people telling stories) would be considered humanities research. Projects that analyze the data in courthouse records of early settlers would be considered social sciences research. Projects that use observational techniques, such as attempts to determine why wolves left Yellowstone, are social science research projects.

Sociologists, archeologists, and anthropologists all do social science research. Since social scientists use survey research, they are likely to use areas on the Web that post data sets, such as that used for the Lou Harris polls. Social scientists use either the *APA Style Guide* (see Chapter 8) or the *Chicago Manual of Style*, published by the University of Chicago Press.[1] Research papers in the social sciences often include headings and subheadings, such as the headings and subheadings used in this text to indicate divisions of each chapter. The headings in social science papers are often standard ones: abstract, introduction, methods, results and discussion, and conclusion. Below are some key sites to explore for social science projects:

Coombs Collection
http://coombs.anu.edu/au/WWWVL-SocSci.html

Social Science—BUBL
http://www.bubl.bath.ac.uk/BUBL/Social_Sciences.html

Infomime: Comprehensive Social Sciences and Humanities Internet Resource Collection
http://infomime.ucr.edu

Social and Behavioral Sciences Information and Services
http://www.uic.edu/depts/lib/socbehav/

Natural Sciences and Mathematics

Researchers in the natural sciences use experimental research methods to look for answers to their research questions. They use both direct experimentation and observation as their primary research techniques, whether they work in the laboratory or in the field (Zimmerman and Rodrigues). For example, if researchers are trying to detect the radiation level in drinking water, they will perform lab experiments designed to isolate the presence of radioactive particles. Below is a list of some comprehensive resources in science and mathematics.

Sci-Central
http://www.scicentral.com/index.html

The Institute of Physics Web Site
http://www.iop.org/

BUBL WWW Subject Tree—Biology
http://www.bubl.bath.ac.uk/BUBL/Biology.html

World Wide Web Virtual Library: Chemistry
http://pluto.njcc.com/~bpapp/chempoin.html

---

[1]See "Documentation: Chicago Style" at <http://www.wisc.edu/writing/handbook/docchicago.html>.

World Wide Web Virtual Library: Math Guide
http://euclid.math.fsu.edu/Science/math.html

New Journal of Physics
http://njp.org

Business

Research in business varies with the field. Some fields of study follow the same documentation guidelines for research in social sciences. Other business areas, in particular those related to statistical analysis, follow guidelines used by mathematics.

The Internet has many valuable business areas. There are discussion lists, file archives, Web sites, and software collections available. A great starting point is the collection of business resources at the Rutgers Library <http://www.libraries.rutgers.edu/rulib/socsci/busi/business.html>. Along with library and Web resources, this list includes the following kinds of sources:

- Dictionaries and encyclopedias
- Electronic texts
- Economic data sources
- Financial data sources
- News sources and electronic journals

One problem in using business resources on the Internet is that they change frequently. Massachusetts Institute of Technology (MIT) keeps an updated reference service at <http://tns-www.lcs.mit.edu/commerc.html>. This listing provides users with the location of new resources. Another problem with business resources is that they are often sponsored by businesses rather than universities. The information on each site must be evaluated carefully for bias. For example, the sites you locate on the Web for E-commerce (see Figure 4.3) might not be the best place to start if you are trying to locate a standard source in this new financial field. Rather, you might start with ABI Inform, a proprietary database where you can find scholarly journals on your topic.

You can find many business journals on the Web by searching for "business journals" with a search engine. You will find business journals from cities across the world.

Here is a list of some business sites you can explore on the Web:

BUBL WWW Subject Tree—Business
http://www.bubl.bath.ac.uk/BUBL/Business.html

The General Accounting Office
Gopher://wiretap.spies.com

CNN Financial News
http://cnnfn.com/

FIGURE 4.3 Results of search for electronic commerce.

Dow Jones Directory
http://www.dowjones.com/

Latin American Information
Gopher://info.lanic.utexas.edu 70

Canadian Information
Gopher://talon.staatcan.ca

***Wall Street Journal* Interactive Edition**
http://www.wsj.com/

Many academic journals and newspapers in the business field are available on the Web. Here are a couple of examples:

Blackwell Publishers
http://www.blackwellpublishers.co.uk

Carfax Publishers (Management and Business)
http://www.carfax.co.uk

Education

Educators from the kindergarten level to the university have been actively developing sites for research and teaching. Teachers of grades K–12 use the Internet to locate lesson plans, to collaborate with other classroom teachers, and to create and advertise Web projects of their own. College and university students and professors use Web sites for research and for display of information about their programs. The sites listed here focus primarily on K–12 education and are most useful for education majors or teachers. Educators follow either MLA or APA style guides, depending on their subject-area specialties (e.g., science educators follow APA, but language arts specialists follow MLA). Distance education specialists use the Web to publish results of their work as well as to explore one another's Web sites to locate resources that can be shared (e.g., course evaluation forms or tutorials on specific kinds of software).

Ask Eric Virtual Library
http://ericir.syr.edu/Virtual

BUBL Subject Tree—Education
http://www.bubl.bath.ac.uk/BUBL/Education.html

Yale University: Subject Guides for Education
http://www.library.yale.edu/socsci/subjguides/education.html

Engineering

Engineering majors often have little room in the curriculum for writing courses. But they are often expected to use writing well when they complete senior research projects or when they do their internships. And they are almost certain to be asked to complete writing tasks such as research reports when they are working as engineering professionals. Technical writing areas on the Web may be useful to anyone doing a research project for an engineering course. Of course, background information for many topics may be located on the Web. Here are some samples of the kinds of information available:

A Guide to Engineering Information on the Internet
http://www.eevl.ac.uk/workbook.html

Edinburgh Engineering Virtual Library (EEVL)
http://www.eevl.ac.uk/

Institute for Mechanical Engineers
http://www.imeche.org.uk/imeche2/default.htm

The Engineering Zone
http://www.geocities.com/CapeCanaveral/Lab/2549/design.htm

Manufacturing Engineering Resources
http://marg.ntu.ac.uk/resources.html

The Scholes Library Engineering and Science Page
http://scholes.alfred.edu/EandS.html

Links to Engineering and IT Related Services
http://www.iee.org.uk/Misc/otherwww.htm

CONCLUSION

This chapter has given you an overview of how to use search tools and subject collections to locate sources in your disciplines. When you locate subject guides, look carefully. Many of them include links to other than just Web resources. For example, a search for academic journals in history turned up a resource for popular magazines about history: The History Net <http://www.thehistorynet.com/>.

Always remember to explore all sources available to you in your library and on the Web. Just because you have located an excellent book on your topic doesn't mean that your research project would not be enhanced by further exploration of database and Web sources. Nor should you overlook the possibility of interviewing experts in your field—perhaps through e-mail (see Chapter 6). You need to locate the best information available on your topic, and that will almost always involve a mix of resources. As new search tools and new subject collections are developed, it will be easier for you to keep track of Web sites in your field. To keep up with resources in your discipline, bookmark the subject-area collections of your choice, and return to them regularly to check for updates.

EXERCISES

1. Using the list of resources in the book as a starting point, develop a more extensive list of resources in your field. Post this list to the "Web Links" section of the Companion Web site for this book <http://www.prenhall.com/rodrigues>.
2. If the best resources in your discipline relate to the topic of your paper, explain why they are helpful.
3. Make a list of any sources you find useful for your paper.
4. Return to your list after you have read Chapter 5 and evaluate your sources as well as the resources in your field.

Evaluating Sources

After completing this chapter, you should be able to do the following:

■ Determine whether the sources you have located are the best possible ones for your topic.

■ Evaluate sources differently in preliminary and later stages of the research process.

■ Be able to determine whether a source is valid in and of itself.

■ Determine whether that source is valid for your research paper.

■ Note potential bias in Web sources based on the URL.

As you work on your research paper, you continue to learn more about a given topic. Your knowledge of the topic is, however, only as sound as the sources you use. Your goal should be to locate authoritative, accurate, unbiased, and current information on your topic—not always an easy task—since to get a good idea of what is available in your field, you need to force yourself to search widely—shuttling between library and Web as needed.

This process takes time and commitment. Plan to spend several weeks locating and doing a preliminary evaluation of your sources before you begin drafting. Gather both Web sources and library sources so that you develop a sense of the range of information available on your topic. Before you begin, evaluate your information needs by answering the following questions:

What do I know about my topic?
What do I need to learn?
What kinds of sources are most likely to help me?
What exactly am I looking for?
What type of Internet resource is likely to help?
What kinds of library resources are likely to help?

EVALUATING INFORMATION:
THE EARLY STAGES OF A RESEARCH PROJECT

Your goal at the outset of a project is to develop a good understanding of your topic. People have different reasons for evaluating information resources. You need to be clear about the purpose of your evaluation.

During the early stages of information gathering, you want to sort and sift quickly. You can gather sources and read them quickly, to get a sense of the topic, but don't take notes. Until you have read widely on your topic, you cannot possibly know how good your sources are.

It is important to evaluate *all* your sources, both as you proceed and then again before you determine whether to use the source in your research paper. When you locate a possible source on your topic, you need to evaluate the information. Here is a list of questions you can use to get started:

Content Criteria

1. Is the source valid? Factual? That is, do you have reason to think that it is accurate information?
2. Is the topic treated thoroughly?
3. Is the treatment biased? If the author acknowledges the bias, you will have an easier time deciding whether or not to use the source. The problem is that many authors do not admit their biases; information is often put on the Web for the sole purpose of promoting a particular point of view; thus, many sites have "hidden agendas." Always check to see if you can learn more about the organization that sponsors the Web site.

Currency

1. Is your information current? Avoid out-of-date books or journal articles, or Web sites, unless you use the sources to establish a point. (For example, you may want to demonstrate what books in the early part of the century said about your topic.)

Source of Publication

1. Is the author an expert on your topic? Find out something about the author. What are the author's credentials? Check the author's Web page to see if he or she has published widely in the field. Check the bibliography or references the author includes. Do these sources appear to be current? Authoritative?
2. Is the source reliable? If you used a scholarly source (a source from an academic press or from an educational institution), it is likely to be reliable. If it is a popular source, you need to be sure that you are using the best source on your topic.

Coverage

1. How complete or extensive is the coverage of the topic? You may be able to use a source that doesn't cover a topic thoroughly, but be sure to supplement it with other sources.
2. Does the source include specific detail?

Any given source you find is not necessarily valuable for your topic: it may be overly biased, it may be out of date, and it may not have been published by a reputable press. Learning which sources are the most appropriate for your paper comes later in the research process, but this is possible only if you have done a good job sorting and sifting early on.

Preliminary Evaluation of Web Sources

You can weed out many sources quickly by learning what to look for in a "good" source and what to avoid. In addition, be aware of some ways to evaluate Internet sources.

Initial Evaluation of Web Sources

■ Check to see if there is a tilde (~) in the URL, which often means that the information is part of someone's personal Web site. Even if the person is part of a respected university, that person's views may be biased and unauthoritative. Personal sites may also contain students' college research papers—not usually sources you should cite.

■ Check the URL to see if it ends in edu, com, gov, or org. Different types of valuable information can be found on any of these sites, but being aware of the type of site you are looking at can help you make a judgment. For example, if you are investigating the status of medical research on arthritis, you may not want to cite information that you find at the Web site for a pharmaceutical company (see Practice Box in this chapter).

■ Examine the style of writing and the level to which it has been edited. If you find incoherent passages and occasional grammar or punctuation errors, you should be wary.

■ Look at the date the site was created or last updated. If the site is out of date, you can eliminate the site as soon as you see it listed in the search engine's report.

■ Note the relationship between author and publisher. For example, if the author is a university professor, and the source was published on a commercial Web site, ask why. Scholarly articles are more likely to be published at an educational site or at the site of an academic publisher.

One of the biggest problems many students have is trying to use sources that are simply not meaty enough to provide them with in-depth information on a topic. Sometimes, even an out-of-date book on a topic can provide a more thorough introduction than a cursory Web page. Do not use a source merely because it is the most convenient one. Determine whether your topic requires that you use a more authoritative or thorough source than is available on the Web.

Determining Whether the Journal or Magazine Is Appropriate for Your Topic

The terms "journal" and "magazine" are sometimes used interchangeably, but research librarians make a distinction that you should be aware of. Magazines generally are aimed at a general reader, the so-called popular press. Journals are typically aimed at the more academic or scholarly reader. Another distinction worth noting is that magazines do not always have volume and issue numbers, and as a result citation style for magazines is different than citation style for journals (see Chapter 8).

Journals vary, too. Sometimes an entire volume—a year's worth of issues usually—is paginated simultaneously. Other times, each issue has its own pagination. Citation styles for these two variants of journals are also different (see Chapter 8).

Is the Journal Popular or Scholarly?

How can you tell whether a given publication is an academic or a popular magazine or journal? Some guidelines are included in Figure 5.1. For additional information, see "How Can You Tell the Difference?" from Cornell University Library <http://www.library.cornell.edu/okuref/research/skill20.html>.

An increasing number of journals that have migrated to the Web have developed an online version of the journal that differs somewhat from the print counterpart. Some of these journals are scholarly journals; others are popular journals. Your research paper topic and the demands your teacher or employer have given you will determine the extent to which you can use Web journals.

Scholarly Article	Popular Article
Aimed at a college-educated reader—often one with an advanced degree.	Aimed at the general reader.
Uses citations to document sources.	Often refers to information without giving any indication of the source.
Uses academic language.	Uses popular language.
Often includes charts and graphs.	May contain many pictures.

FIGURE 5.1 Scholarly and popular articles.

Is an Online Journal Appropriate?

Electronic versions of journals may be lacking in terms of articles, images, graphics, or citations. Although electronic products may offer more information and articles than a library can acquire through print subscriptions, libraries seeking to replace their print subscriptions with electronic alternatives need to consider that the options are not necessarily equivalent.

Take time to determine whether the online journal is a serious undertaking or a casual production. Some "zines" (online magazines) depend on volunteers and are not monitored for consistency.

The Importance of Exploring Varied Sources

Don't just start taking notes. You have to read awhile before you can develop a sense of the range of information available or before you can spot bias. You may locate a useful source early in your research process, one that gives you adequate background on your topic. But should you cite this source in your paper? You cannot evaluate a source fairly until you know what other sources are available.

Keep the purpose of your research in mind as you work on your research paper. Are you investigating an issue? Examining different viewpoints? Or arguing a point? Your selection of sources is related to your research questions and your purpose for researching. When you are drafting your paper, you will want to select from your collection of credible sources those that best further your investigation or support your argument. Only when you determine how you will *use* a source in your paper will you be able to determine whether it is the best source possible for that purpose. Are you going to use a student interview to establish a point about local school violence? If so, your source may be better than a scholarly article at that point in your draft.

EVALUATION AT THE DRAFTING PHASE

Your goal is to sort through these sources and use only the best of what you find. Assuming you have done some preliminary sorting, you will develop key questions like the ones in the next paragraph. Many students who have located information about their topics with the Web are amazed to discover the different level of sophistication and the depth of analysis of issues in the books and journals they locate.

You can get reasonably good results on the Web without knowing a lot about searching, but when you use commercial databases, you need to understand that they are targeted toward more professional users and may not be as easy to use. That's why it is important to explore all the databases available to you so that you can locate the five or six that have the most useful information for your field or for the topics in which you are most interested. Here are some questions to ask if you are about to start drafting your research paper:

■ Is the information you have located relevant to your topic and to your argument? Just because a source is valid does not mean it is appropriate for your topic.

■ Does your source fit the context of your paper?

■ Is your source the best source you can find on the topic? Unless you have collected more sources than you can use, you won't know the answer to this question.

■ Is your source the right type of source for your topic? For example, you probably need primary sources if you are exploring a legal issue. You can find state and federal court cases on the Web.

■ Have you explored your topic thoroughly? You typically need more thorough coverage of a topic than that provided by a Web source.

■ Have you examined the point of view of your source? You need to be sure that the point of view expressed in your source is compatible with the point you are making in your paper.

Although subscription databases are more likely to contain useful sources of information for many of your topics, do not assume that all journals you locate through a database are good sources. Consider issues such as the following:

■ When was the database updated?

■ Do I have to search a print index for earlier titles?

■ Are there better sources in the library that are not available online?

Determining What Kinds of Sources to Explore

Sometimes it is not a matter of evaluation, but rather a matter of knowing where to go to look for a topic. In "Books, Web sites, or Journal? The Information Cycle" <http://www.farmingdale.edu/CampusPages/ComputingAndLibrary/Library/inflow.html#>, the librarians at Greenley Library of SUNY Farmingdale look at topics in the context of when they happened. They suggest that you use time as a guideline to help you determine whether a source is appropriate for your topic. Ask the following question: When did events related to my topic occur? Your answer will often determine where you look for information.

If the events are recent, the Web may be appropriate. If the events took place several years ago, the library is probably a better starting point.

If the event *just* happened, the Web is likely to be a good source of information, along with newspapers, television, and radio. A week later, however, a better source—one where the author has perhaps had more time to reflect on and digest the information—might be a popular magazine. Six months later, a good place to locate information might be in a peer-reviewed academic journal on the topic; over time, books on the topic may prove even better sources of information, for they allow in-depth coverage of a topic. Of course, all of theses sources may be biased for they contain the author's slant on the topic and they may be sponsored by a professional organization or political group

PRACTICE BOX

What can you tell about a Web site based on its URL? If you remember the following distinctions between "domain names" (the three letters after the period in a URL that refer to the domain or origin of the computer server that feeds the page to the Web), you will have good starting points for evaluating Web sites.

Government site	.gov	U.S. government
Military site	.mil	military organization of the U.S. government
Company site	.com	company pages or individuals who have their informational pages located on a site such as America Online <www.aol.com>
Network Services	.net	organization that administers or provides network connection services
Educational site	.edu	four-year college or similar educational institution (Educational institutions below four-year colleges are encouraged to use the geographic "us" top-level domain name.)
Organization	.org	nonprofit organizations and other similar groups
Country Codes	au, uk, ca	Australia, United Kingdom, and Canada

For a complete list of domain names by country code, see "List of Domain Suffixes" at <http://www.currents.net/resources/dictionary/domains.html>.

What conclusions can be made about the following sources on the basis of their URLs?

1. http://www.sierraclub.org
2. http://thomas.loc.gov
3. http://www.phil.indiana.edu/ejap/1998/contents98.html
4. http://www.amnesty.org
5. http://www.prenhall.com
6. http://www.austin.cc.tx.us

with its own perspective or agenda. After more time goes by, the event may be included in reference books, which generally try to be neutral but which may also have hidden or overt biases and other limitations.

CONCLUSION

After you locate a source, take time to evaluate it. Evaluation is a crucial step in the research process. Although there are differences in the way you evaluate library sources and Web sources, the basic criteria are the same.

The techniques you use for evaluating Web sources and print sources have much in common, for the basic question you are asking yourself of each source is this: Will the source be credible for *my* purposes in *my* paper? In other words, will the source help you explain your point or demonstrate that your work makes a contribution to a reader's growing understanding of your topic?

At first, you may find it difficult to determine whether sources you locate are valid. Over time, however, most students become expert at "sniffing" out the problems. With experience, researchers develop a second sense for spotting inaccurate sources. It may be that inexperienced Web surfers simply have not yet learned how to read the sign system of the Web. Over time, you will notice things like the domain names that help indicate bias, a clue that initially went unobserved and undetected.

EXERCISES

1. Develop a notation system to indicate whether your sources appear to be: (1) valid in and of themselves and (2) valid in the context of your paper. Include all sources—print and online—in your evaluation.

2. Bring several sources with you to class. Evaluate your classmates' sources using the preliminary evaluation criteria referred to in this chapter. Which sources do you think are valid or invalid in isolation? Are there any instances where the sources, though invalid in isolation, might be useful in context?

3. When you have finished drafts of your papers, repeat this exercise. Have you or your classmates eliminated any sources that appeared to be useful when you examined them in isolation?

4. Find a set of sources that are not valid. Explain to your classmates your reasons for coming to that conclusion.

E-mail, Newsgroups, Forums, and Listservs as Research Tools

After completing this chapter, you should be able to do the following:

■ Use the following tools to gather resources: e-mail, newsgroups, listservs (mailing lists), and forums.

■ Understand appropriate netiquette in using these tools.

E-mail (electronic mail), mailing lists (e-mail to a group of people with some common interest), and newsgroups (discussion groups on a wide variety of topics and issues) can all be used as research tools. E-mail allows you to write messages to people throughout the world who are specialists on your subject; mailing lists help researchers and specialists on specific topics (as well as students conducting research) to share ideas quickly; and newsgroups, using programs that function like bulletin boards, enable groups of people, often experts on their topics, to post messages called *articles* to topical areas that can be searched for later retrieval. Forums are designed to allow topics and subtopics to be discussed by anyone who accesses the forum.

Most Web browsers (programs that allow you to jump from one Web site to another) are all-purpose tools. That is, not only can you navigate from site to site on the Internet with these browsers, but you can also read newsgroups or access e-mail directly from them. An advantage to using mail from within a browser is that you can attach pages that you find on the Web in your messages and share them with friends or fellow researchers. Likewise, you can paste URLs into your messages and make it possible for recipients to visit Web sites that you refer to in your message. A disadvantage to using e-mail from within a browser is that its e-mail software may be inferior to standard e-mail software.

As you read each section that follows, explore the possibilities at your local site. Examine the features of your browser. If the browser used at your site does not integrate e-mail and newsgroups, you might want to find out if you can install a different browser on your computer.

E-MAIL

Remember that our purpose here is to examine the uses of e-mail as a research tool. Because e-mail can travel across the country—or the world—in a matter of seconds, you can get quick responses if the person to whom you wrote checks his or her mail regularly.

If you use e-mail effectively, you can gather up-to-the-moment information about your topic from experts whose e-mail addresses are available to you. Becoming an effective e-mail user, however, means that you need to understand the conventions of addressing and composing e-mail, write messages that are concise and to the point, and know what to do with the answers you receive.

Write e-mail messages to people who may be experts in the subject you are researching with your reader in mind. Because the person you are writing to may be an expert, it is possible that he or she may have very limited time for reading and responding to your message, so use techniques that are most likely to get the kind of response you want. Be polite, yet scholarly. Show your reader that you care about the topic and that you have done some preliminary reading before writing your message of inquiry. Show the reader that you respect his or her time by keeping your query short and direct. Try to end your message with a clear indication of what you want the reader to do as a result of your message.

Using E-mail for Data Gathering: Questions to Ask

Whether you use e-mail for personal communication or for research, you should take some time to learn the conventions of e-mail use. For each research project, ask yourself these questions:

■ Is e-mail the appropriate genre to use for your research inquiries? Would a letter be more appropriate? It is very likely that a person whose e-mail address you can find on the Web is also a person who uses e-mail regularly and so may respond to your query. If you cannot find the e-mail address of the person you are searching for and if that person's address does not appear on a web site such as Excite's People finder <http://www.excite.com/reference/people_finder>, then you may want to write a letter in care of the publisher who published the article or book that you read.

■ How can you find e-mail addresses of specialists on your topic? Consider joining a mailing list on the topic. After reading its messages for several days, you will begin to notice that respondents often defer to several people—the specialists on that list. In addition, various search engines have tools for finding the e-mail addresses of individuals, so after finding the name of an expert in your reading, one you would like to correspond with, you can search for that person's e-mail address. For example, Lycos has a

"People Finder" <http://www.whowhere.lycos.com>, and other search engines also have sites to search for e-mail addresses by people's names. And some people allow their e-mail addresses to be used in their role of expert. For example, one Web site designed to link you with experts is at <http://www.askanexpert.com/askanexpert/cat.shtml>. There, you can begin searching by categories, and then you can send a question directly to the person who has volunteered to be listed. The E-Mail Address Book is helpful when looking for addresses of people on America Online, Prodigy, or CompuServ. If you know an expert is located at a particular university, you can usually go to that university's home page and use the "Whois" database to find the e-mail address. If the expert has his or her own Web page, then you might be able to use Who's Who Online or Personal Pages Worldwide. Finally, many specific disciplines have their own address sites, such as the Worldwide Directory of Finance Faculty, Directory of Economists, Find Arts, Home Page of Astronomers, Directory of Biologists, Directories of Historians, West's Legal Directory, Librarian's Home Pages, Who's Online—Mathematicians, Media E-mail Addresses, Address Directory for Politicians of the World, The Electronic Activist, and the Directory of Theater Professionals on the Internet.

■ When is it more important to call or visit an expert rather than to send an e-mail? That may be a decision that you have to make based upon your best judgment, but if you do not know the person, writing first for an appointment is an acceptable procedure.

E-mail programs usually allow you to create folders for different topics. If your e-mail program has this capability, learn how to use it. Organizing your e-mail in folders according to topics can help you find messages you want to incorporate into your research papers or reports. (See Chapter 7 for a discussion of ways to organize notes for research.)

The Etiquette of E-mail: Netiquette

As sincere as your e-mail request for information may be, you increase the chances that the person whom you wrote to will not respond if you violate some of the standard etiquette rules for using e-mail, i.e., "netiquette." Being aware of netiquette, you are more likely to get a response from the expert you write to, especially if that expert does not know you personally. Since e-mail is still a new form of writing for many people, the conventions are still evolving. As with other forms of written communication, e-mail conventions may vary from one context to another.

If you are sending e-mail to a friend, you may be able to ignore the conventions of e-mail. So, as with other forms of audience, it is important that you know your audience when you send e-mail messages. Below are a set of guidelines that can help you increase the chances of receiving the type of response you seek. While it is best to follow these, remember that they are only guidelines, not absolute rules.

- Keep messages to one screen in length. Longer messages are harder for the reader to keep in mind and may require the reader to scroll back and forth between screens to follow your message well. The longer and more complex the message, the more scrolling. The more scrolling, the less likely a busy reader is to finish the message, and, therefore, the less likely he or she may respond to your inquiry.

- Try to write about only one topic in each e-mail message. It is difficult for readers to remember what you asked or said if you write about more than one topic.

- Do not type everything in capital letters. First, IT APPEARS AS THOUGH YOU ARE SHOUTING! NO E-MAIL READER LIKES TO BE YELLED AT! But second, and more importantly, readability research has shown that readers can process text more easily if the text contains both upper- and lowercase letters than if it is all uppercase.

- Let the reader know the purpose of the message immediately. This focuses the reader's mind on what the task will be. And if the reader is busy or impatient, he or she might not want to guess at why you are writing before coming to the end of your message. End your message by politely restating the purpose of the inquiry, perhaps as part of your thanking the reader for his or her help.

- Vary your e-mail style according to your audience. E-mail tends to be an informal way of writing, and if you have been writing to friends or colleagues before, you may unconsciously be as casual with a stranger as with a friend. Don't be. When you write to experts whom you do not know, you do not want to offend them. If you have designed some clever signature block for e-mail that you use normally, you may want to remove it before writing to a stranger. However, a formal signature block with your name, address, and telephone number is permissible.

- Reread your message before you send it to correct any accidental errors you may have made in typing it, even though experienced e-mail users tend to tolerate errors in e-mail more than they do in letters. Several reasons explain why errors in e-mail are more easily tolerated: (1) e-mail is often written rapidly (and is more like talking than writing), so mistakes are often made because of fast typing; (2) many e-mail systems do not have spell-checkers like word processing programs have; and (3) simple e-mail programs may not adjust line lengths when corrections are made, causing people not to correct their mistakes. Nevertheless, because you want to make a good first impression and increase your chances of getting the response you want, if you see errors and can correct them, do.

- When replying to e-mail, do not copy the entire message into your response unless you think the sender will need a reminder of what the e-mail is about. If you can summarize the original e-mail rather than copy it, that is even better. Or you can copy a portion of the original e-mail that encapsulates the purpose of the entire e-mail.

- Do not expect an immediate response. Many people are very busy and may not get to your message immediately. Wait a few days before sending a follow-up e-mail message and when you do, treat the person you are e-mailing as politely as you would anyone else.

■ If you plan to copy the e-mail message that you receive to another person, let the sender know. E-mail is open to the public, so any message you or another person writes can be copied immediately, but it does not hurt to treat e-mail messages that you receive as confidential information. Since you will be using e-mail for your research, letting the person you are writing to know that you are planning to use the information as part of your research would be the respectful thing to do.

Finally, while this is not strictly a matter of etiquette, do use reasonable caution in writing e-mail messages, for no e-mail message is truly secure. You can never be certain that your e-mail message will not be read by someone whom you do not want to see it, for it may be stored some place that others can read it. Therefore, do not write anything that you do not want someone other than your intended reader to see. Some people recommend that you not write anything that you would not want revealed in a court of law. While that caution may be extreme, it does serve to remind us all that we must be cautious not to libel others or say anything that might embarrass us if read by others whom we did not intend to read it.

Creating and Sending E-mail Messages to Request Information

To create an e-mail message, follow the directions for the e-mail program that you use. The suggestions that follow are intended to make your research more effective.

Note the address of the person to whom you are sending the e-mail. E-mail addresses are usually in the form: user@host.domain. The **user** is the e-mail name of the recipient or the names of a distribution list that, in turn, sends mail to many users. Be aware that, if you receive a message from an individual, that message may have been sent through a distribution list. If you reply to a message from a listserv, you will send your message to everyone on the list, whether you want to or not. **Host.domain** is the full name and address of the host or server computer on which the user has an e-mail account. Some are more complex than others, and any mistake in typing the address will result in your message not going where you want it to go.

The last three letters of the address let you know the general type of organization that controls the server on which the sender has an e-mail account. Notice the following:

.edu means that the sender is writing from an educational location or server
.com means that the sender is using a commercial location or server
.gov means that the group server in the address is a government server
.org stands for a formal organization or group server

You may want to copy the message to yourself so that you can document having sent the message and remember exactly what it was that you wrote.

Most e-mail programs enable you to do so by clicking on the **To** box to find options such as **cc**. You can also send blind copies, or copies that the receiver will not know that you copied, by choosing **bc** from your options. But many people believe it is improper etiquette or even unethical to copy a message without letting the receiver know.

The subject line also serves an important function for e-mail research, allowing you to file and keep track of messages regarding your topics. Therefore, it is important that you identify the subject as accurately and concisely as you can. Doing so tells your reader the topic you are writing about, and it later can help you identify the message when you want to refer to it. So, for example, if you are writing to someone about the etiquette of e-mail messages, the subject "computer use" would be too broad, and therefore, vague and not useful. The subject "computer etiquette" would be more exact.

Here is an example of what a good e-mail inquiry sent to an expert whom you don't know might look like:

To: Hisname@lawfirm.com

From: Jdoesmith@stateuniv.edu

Cc: Jdoesmith@stateuniv.edu

Subject: E-mail Legal Risk

Can you give me your advice on the conditions under which a person can legally be held accountable for what that person writes in an e-mail? I am a student in a Business Law course at the State University, and I am writing a research paper on the ways e-mail messages can be used as evidence in court. I have read several articles that advise readers not to write anything in e-mail messages that they would not want to have revealed in court, but I want to learn what kinds of messages specifically would put a person at risk in a court trial. The article in * Newsworld Magazine * mentioned you as an expert, so that is why I am writing to you. I appreciate how busy you may be and any guidance you may be able to give me regarding the legal risks of e-mail.

Jane Doesmith

Notice that the writer indicated that she had already done some research before actually writing to the expert, even referring to the source that led her to write to him. The request is fairly specific, so the expert does not have to use valuable time trying to determine exactly what the writer wants.

Tom Rocklin quotes an e-mail message he once received that did not inspire him to write back to the sender:

Subject: Learning Opportunities in a Digital Age

I am writing a paper on how computers are used in the health field. I would like to cite some examples of new procedures used with the aid of the computer, as well as how the health field has benefited from computers and will benefit in the future. Can you help me? I appreciate your time.

Anne (not her real name)

This request is too broad, does not indicate that the writer has done any preliminary research whatsoever, and does not indicate why the writer has sent the request to Rocklin at all. If it received no response, that should not be a surprise.

Attaching Documents to E-mail Messages

Most e-mail programs will allow you to attach documents to your e-mail messages when you want to send someone a document or a Web site address that is worth investigating. Typically, all you have to do is go to the e-mail program, click on the icon that indicates attachment, and then follow the directions that appear in a pop-up box. This is particularly valuable when you are not at your home computer but have access to an e-mail program. You can capture or attach the document or Web site address that you want and send it to yourself at your home computer. When you arrive home, you simply open the e-mail message that you sent yourself and click on the attachment. Figure 6.1 shows what one attachment pop-up box looks like just before the writer selected the particular file that he wanted to send to himself.

Saving and Filing E-mail Messages

If you are conducting research by sending and receiving e-mail messages, you will want to file the messages you receive and sometimes the messages that you send. Most e-mail programs provide you with at least two options for saving your e-mail messages: you can either (1) save the e-mail as an e-mail message within the e-mail program or (2) save the e-mail as a regular word processing file in your word processing program.

To save the e-mail message as an e-mail message, you can go to the part of your e-mail program that may be called **File**, click on it, and then save the e-mail message in a folder that you create. For efficiency, you may want to create a folder called *research paper* or whatever the topic of your research is and then create subfolders within that main folder for the subcategories of your research. As you learn more about your subject, you may decide that the folder subcategories that you originally created are no longer appropriate or need to be recategorized in some manner. If that is the case, then all you have to do is create folders for the new subcategories and copy your e-mail messages from

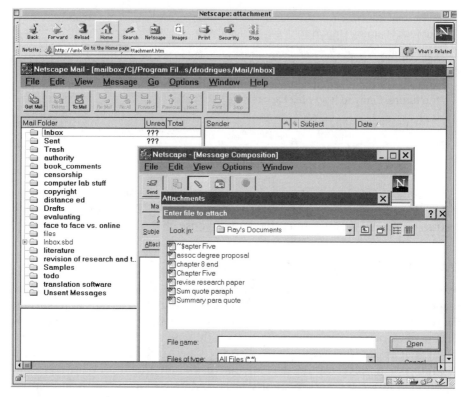

FIGURE 6.1 The attachment box within Netscape Mail.

one folder to another, deleting the original only after completing your entire copying process. (Remember an important suggestion from word processing experts: add information or a new version first; delete last.)

For purposes of research, though, saving your e-mail messages in your e-mail program may not be the better choice, for you cannot manipulate them as easily as you can if you save them in your word processing program. So it is preferable to copy your e-mail messages when you receive them and save them directly in your word processing program. You can still save the messages in directories and subdirectories based upon the subcategories of your research. Not only can you move them around just as you could in your e-mail program, but more importantly, you can cut and paste portions into your research paper draft, editing the information as you want, but keeping the original in its original form. By not deleting the original e-mail message, when you cite the sources of your information from e-mail messages, you can cite the original sender and date of the message.

PRACTICE BOX

1. Practice sending e-mail messages back and forth between other members of your class and your professor. Practice saving your e-mails into your e-mail program file area. After you have saved a few, practice organizing them into folders.

2. Search for several of the various directories of addresses on the Web. As you find and go to each, notice what the information does and does not say about the individual. Can you determine whether the individual is one who might answer a particular question of yours or if the information provided is too little? You will not want to write at random to people you do not know.

3. Find the name of an individual who should be an expert in the book or article that you have. Try finding an e-mail address for that person. If you cannot find that person, look for another. Try finding the e-mail address of someone who is in the current news or entertainment industry. Do not write to that person unless you have a legitimate reason for doing so, but do share your successes and failures at locating addresses with your classmates. Then, as a class, develop your own set of guidelines for finding e-mail addresses on the Web.

4. If you were an expert in a particular topic, what kind of e-mail inquiry would you be likely to respond to? What characteristics of an e-mail inquiry would cause you not to respond to it?

MAILING LISTS

What is a mailing list? It is a system for sending e-mail to a group of people who are interested in a common topic. The "list" consists of computerized lists of electronic addresses. A computer referred to as a listserver distributes mail sent to people who have joined the mailing list, which is run by a computer program. Two of the most popular mailing list programs are LISTSERV by Eric Thomas and LISTPROC by Anastasio Kotsikonas. Mailing lists are more or less focused discussions on topics from popular fads and entertainment to politics, business, educational practices, and almost anything imaginable. Messages sent are received by all subscribers to the list, i.e., the people who send and receive messages to and from each other. This section shows you how to subscribe to a list, use the list in an appropriate manner, and use the list for research purposes.

Subscribing to a Mailing List

To subscribe to a list, send a simple request to an address in the form: <list-request@hostname>

To: listserv@ncte.org

Do not write anything in the "subject" line, but do write the following in the message portion of the e-mail:

Subscribe <listname> <yourfirstname yourlastname>

Do not write your full e-mail address here, just your name. For example:

Subscribe ncte-talk Dawn Rodrigues

The reason for not writing a subject name, your full e-mail address, or anything else is simple: what you are doing is sending a message to the computer server that maintains the list, not to a person who will read your message and not to any of the other people on the mail list. The computer adds you to the list of subscribers. In less than a day, you should receive a return message such as the following from the server:

You have been successfully added to the list NCTE-talk

Later, if you want to unsubscribe (be removed from the mailing addresses on the list), you will also have to communicate to the computer server at the appropriate address. If you simply ask to be removed by sending a message to the list itself, you will have sent the message to all the other recipients of the e-mail messages, and nothing will happen. That is, the computer server will not act on your request, but others might write to you telling you how to unsubscribe or sign off. And you can hope that they use appropriate netiquette in doing so.

Besides telling you that you have been successfully added to the list that you want to subscribe to, the computer program will send you a message with appropriate commands that you can use while on this particular list. Most commands will be the same from list to list, but some will vary, so you should save these commands where you can easily find them when you need them, such as in a separate folder or directory for list commands.

The following is a list of possible LISTSERV commands that you can use. (Note: send these commands to the administrative address of the list, not the address where you send your e-mails.)

Info	Get detailed information files
List	Get a description of all lists (from this server)

SUBscribe	Subscribe to a list listname <full_name> (Note: You can type either **sub** or **subscribe**.)
SIGNOFF	Sign off from a list (or sometimes **UNSUB**scribe)
REView	Review the list of subscribers
STATslistname	Review list statistics
Query	Query or ask for personal distribution options for this list
SET listname	Set personal distribution options <options>
INDex filelist_name	Obtain a list of LISTSERV files
GET filename	Obtain a file from LISTSERV filetype
REGister	Tell LISTSERV about your name: full_name OFF

The following is a list of possible LISTPROC commands that you can use:

Sub or **subscribe**	to subscribe to the list
Signoff	to unsubscribe from the list
Info	to get more information about the list
Review	to get a list of all the subscribers
Help	to get help

Mailing List Basics

When you send a message to a mailing list, you are really sending it to the computer that handles the list. The computer will simply send your message to everyone on the list. If you have questions, you need to write to the owner of the list. When you reply to a message on a mailing list, you can either reply to the author of the message or to everyone subscribing to the list.

Familiarize yourself with the peculiarities of the list to which you subscribe. Find out whether your list is a moderated list, an unmoderated list, or an announcements list. With a moderated list, the list owner reads each message before it is posted; in some cases, the moderator may even introduce a message, perhaps linking it to a previous message or thread of discussion, or he or she may summarize the message if it is too long. With unmoderated lists, every message submitted to the list is posted. Asking a question of or commenting to the owner of the list by sending your message to the list itself may not get any reply at all from the owner, for the owner may not be participating in the list. The third type of list, an announcements list, is simply that, a place where someone places announcements. It is the least valuable type for research purposes.

Learn how your mail program handles list messages. In most mail programs, pressing **reply** sends your message not to the author of the message, but to the entire list. Even experienced mailing list members may accidentally post messages to the entire list when they intend them to go to the owner or only to the person who wrote a particular message. As a newcomer, you may not want to draw attention to your mistakes, so be careful the first few times you send messages to a list.

The Etiquette of Mailing Lists

Each mailing list group develops a culture of its own, with conventions that have evolved gradually over time. If you get involved in a discussion, you should realize that, as a newcomer, you should not try to change the culture of a group. You can, however, observe how other members of the list disagree with one another and notice the consequences. If you do become an established member of a given list, do not let yourself be muzzled by the conventions. Instead, find ways to say what you want to say. Do not assume that the way people behave on one list is automatically acceptable on another. For example, some list owners (the individuals who set up the list) do not want people to "flame," or taunt, one another. On other lists, however, contributors are encouraged to push the limits of a given topic or conversational style.

Just as in writing e-mail messages, some rules of etiquette apply:

- Complete the **subject** area of your message carefully so that subscribers to a list can decide whether they want to read it or delete it without reading it. Some lists have many messages and many discussion threads, so people with little time to spare often have to be selective in what they take time to read.
- If you are new to a mailing list, you may want to introduce yourself before plunging in with a new topic or area of interest. Even when you comment on previous messages the first time, your readers will probably want to know who you are. They will not expect an extensive bibliography, just a sentence explaining that you are a student or work in a particular occupation, if that is pertinent to the topic.
- Sign your name at the end of your messages since not all e-mail programs will show your readers your full name, affiliation, and address. If you can, set up a signature file in your e-mail program: this file will automatically attach to the end of each message your name, affiliation, address, telephone number, and other information you choose. (Note: some writers also attach all sorts of cute things here: sayings, pictures, nicknames, and so forth. If you want to be perceived as serious, do not do that yourself.)
- Generally, before you start sending messages to a list, read what others have been writing. Each list evolves its own personality over time, so if you are entering a list that has been around a while, reading previous messages (see the **INDex filelist_name** command) or reading current messages as they are posted can give you a flavor of the list—the level of expertise of the members, the level of seriousness or frivolity, the ways the list members treat one another's comments. By reading what others write, you can get a sense of the kinds of questions or comments or topics that are appropriate for that particular list.
- If a list has many threads of discussions or topics going on at the same time, it is sometimes useful to start your message by noting what you are writing about. For example, "Jane Doesmith recently argued that impeachment should only be allowed for treason or equally serious offenses by the President. I disagree . . ."

- Contribute something to the list if you take from it. If you are doing research on Web browsers, for example, you might ask, "What is your favorite browser? What characteristics do you like about it?" Offer to send the results of your survey to the members of the list, for they might appreciate your research for their own purposes.

- Respect the time of the other people on the list. Do not write long messages that consume a lot of time to read, and try not to dominate a list by always responding to everything said or by always introducing new topics. A common phenomenon in the lifespan of a list is the following: It begins gradually and grows popular by word of mouth, or word of e-mail, or by being mentioned in a print publication. Then, a small group of people begin to dominate the list. Regardless of the topic, they have to comment on it. Soon, they appear to be carrying on a personal correspondence with each other. And then others drop off the list, leaving the list to those very few.

- Don't flame. Flaming is a term that means insulting the comments or the personality of a writer. It is rude, unnecessary, and can cause a writer to stop sending any messages to the list, perhaps even to unsubscribe. It is one thing to be critical of a person's comments or opinions; it is another to belittle or insult those comments or opinions.

- If someone is rude enough to flame you, don't be upset. Perhaps your comment may have been discussed many times before on the list, so some members may not want to discuss it again (although their flaming behavior is uncalled for). Often someone on the list will correct the flamer for that behavior.

Discussions on e-mail and mailing lists are not always as open as they appear to be. For example, on a list called Techwri-L—a list provided for technical writers—some participants tried to make the list more provocative and less purely technical. They were told to stop. A message with the subject "Off-Topic Issues on Techwri-L" made it clear that certain topics were acceptable and others were not.

Even if you do not plan to get involved in the discussion list, pay attention to what others do and say. The insights you gain by observing conventions on one list will help you cut your learning time in the future. As a beginner to Internet research, you need to realize that you are in a strange land with conventions that you may never have seen before. Take time to get to know the list that you are thinking about sending a message to. Do not write (as did one student): "I'm interested in creative drama. I need information for a paper." You are likely to get a response such as the one she got: "Have you heard of libraries? There are lots of books on that subject." Instead, say something like, "I'm interested in creative drama. I've read several books on the subject and noticed that the authors talk about successful practices, not about difficulties in using creative drama. Have you had any difficulties getting students to participate?"

PRACTICE BOX

1. If possible, practice using a mailing list by creating one for your class or work group. In your first message, post your name and your research interests. (Ask the computer center operators at your school if they will create mailing lists for student groups.) In subsequent messages, respond to one another. Share ideas, discuss issues, probe topics. This kind of informal discussion with people you know can be useful for exploring a topic in depth. It can also give you practice staying with a topic thread and learning how to introduce a new thread. When you are continuing a discussion, say something like, "I want to add a point to the discussion on [specific aspect of the topic]" to help your readers follow the thread. If your readers do not want to read about that, they can delete your message. When you want to change the topic of a discussion, say something like, "I'd like to switch to a different topic at the moment."

2. Experiment with different ways of running a discussion. Select someone to moderate a list for several weeks. Do you prefer a moderated or unmoderated list?

3. Create a classroom file of mailing lists and their topics. As you find a list on a new topic, add your list to that of the rest of the class. Start with the list name and summarize its purpose, e.g., <ncte-talk>, a list for English and language arts teachers and professors. They write about topics like teaching composition or literature or they discuss items of interest to the National Council of Teachers of English.

4. Are the following requests for information effective? Why or why not?

   a. "I am doing research on Internet censorship. Please send me whatever information you have. I have to include Web sources in my paper."

   b. "I have to do a research paper on affirmative action. I have found many sources that argue for it based upon human dignity, making up for past injustices, and so forth, but I can't find any sources that are opposed to affirmative action. Help!"

   c. "I am doing a research paper on copyright laws and read your article that appeared in the On-Line Newsletter regarding guidelines for copying Web pages. I understand that you have considerable experience with issues related to intellectual property and copyright laws. I have been able to locate guidelines to print sources, and I have read guidelines for multimedia or Web sources. But every source I read has a different way of citing Web pages. Can you please tell me what citation style you prefer? Thank you for taking the time to answer my question."

Using Mailing Lists for Research

You may find several places on the Web that will give you access to various mailing lists. One, for example, is **tile.net** at <http://tile.net>. There you can search for lists by category and receive extensive compilings of various lists. When you choose a list, you will be given the address to which you can subscribe. Subscribe to one, and you will soon receive confirmation and any instructions that you need. You may want to narrow your search as much as possible; for example, a recent search for the topic "business" turned up 146 mailing lists, "business marketing" turned up 210, "marketing law" turned up 329 (197 mailing lists, sixty UseNet Newsgroups, eighteen FTP sites, fourteen Internet service companies, and forty computer product vendors). Even "marketing tires" resulted in sixty-four mailing lists.

If you would rather use e-mail to acquire mailing lists, you can order a complete list of Internet mailing lists on your topic by sending a message to the following address: <Listserv@vm1.nodak.edu>. In your message, include the following text: **List global/[your topic]** (e.g., list global/library).

When you determine which mailing lists interest you, subscribe to several lists, for you may find that some lists really do not discuss the topic you need for your research. When you subscribe, you should receive directions on accessing the archives for that list. That is a quick way of determining whether the list is for you, rather than waiting for new messages to appear. If the list is not what you want, simply unsubscribe.

The basic procedures for saving and categorizing e-mail messages can also be used for information that you gather from various lists. You can save the messages as e-mail files or copy them and save them as word processing files. By saving the entire e-mail message that you receive from a list, you can cite it as a source when you need to document the information that you include in your research paper. If you do not want to save an entire message because it is more than you need, do not forget to still save the source information—the sender, date, and subject. The information contained in the electronic header to an e-mail message gives you the date and time, the e-mail address of the sender, and the subject, as well as information on the e-mail's path that you won't need. You can copy all that information when you save your e-mail messages. By labeling the messages as accurately as possible and placing them in appropriate directories and subdirectories, when you begin to write your research paper, you will already have a good organization of information and notes.

USING NEWSGROUPS FOR RESEARCH

In contrast to a mailing list, a newsgroup is a "bulletin board" where individual messages are posted. Instead of messages coming directly to your mailbox, news messages go directly to the computer that hosts the news software. To read news messages, you have to go to the newsgroup to find out what has been posted. This is a normal procedure, unlike using mailing lists, where you have to access the archives to read previous messages. Some people prefer mailing lists; others prefer newsgroups. The advantage of newsgroups is that the messages are not stored on your computer. The disadvantage is that the messages do not stay on the newsgroup bulletin board indefinitely. If you think that you want to use a message in your research paper, you should save it to a file as soon as possible.

Newsgroups are actually run by many computer systems. That is, all the messages do not reside on one central computer. Rather, messages from different people are transferred to whatever computer manages a given topic.

You can locate information for research projects by reading newsgroup messages devoted to your topic. Messages sent to newsgroups sound the same as those posted to mailing lists, for their purpose is similar and some of them coexist as mailing lists.

Newsgroups are organized in a hierarchical fashion, essentially an information tree. You can work your way down through the roots of the tree by selecting from the choices that are given you.

To access newsgroups, you may be able to use your Web browser. One site to begin with is **dejanews**: <http://www.dejanews.com>. Here you can begin by searching categories. For example, begin with the category government. Within that category are the subcategories: countries, general, jobs, law, military, politics, and taxes. Choosing politics gives you the following subcategories: conspiracy, issues, liberalism, libertarian, regional, and socialism. It also gives you a list of political forums and a special discussion group on a current event. If you choose the subcategory regional, you are given the choice of either the subcategory United States or the subcategory United Kingdom. But you also receive a list of regional forums from all over the world. Be aware that not all opinions are the opinions of experts: most are from ordinary people, and their value to your research will depend upon the nature of your topic.

Students in Michael Day's technical writing class at the South Dakota School of Mines and Technology are asked to try to find information for their class projects by writing to experts on their topics. Day encourages students to request information, to answer questions of others on the newsgroup or list, or to gather facts and opinions using a survey or questionnaire. Day explains one successful request:

> One student was writing a proposal on upgrading our school's Auto-
> Cad software and needed information about what version of the soft-
> ware other schools used. . . . He sent in his question to the AutoCad
> discussion list and received 6 responses in the next few days. (157)

Cybersociety: Computer-Mediated Communication and Community includes several chapters about research into UseNet groups. The authors argue that ways of behaving in a UseNet group are self-regulated by the members. In other words, participants tend to correct their own conduct until it fits the norms of the group. Another chapter explores the identity of UseNet groups and finds that even when people have the option of being anonymous, they prefer using their real names.

PRACTICE BOX

1. Compile a list of at least five mailing lists that deal with a topic you are interested in researching. Go to tile.net to begin your search. As you search your way through tile.net, keep a log of all the choices you are given and the ones that you choose. When you subscribe to each mailing list, keep a written record of what each mailing list is about and then summarize the topics that you found the writers actually discussing. If you discover that a mailing list is not appropriate, do not destroy your notes, but keep them, adding to them as you read through the archives of each mailing list to determine whether it is appropriate for your research. When you finish, discuss with others in your class what worked and what did not work in conducting your research using mailing lists.

2. Compile a list of at lease five newsgroups that deal with a topic you are interested in researching. Go to dejanews to begin your search. As you search your way through dejanews, keep a log of all the choices you are given and the ones that you choose. When you subscribe to each mailing list, keep a written record of what each mailing list is about and then summarize the topics that you found the writers actually discussing. If you discover that a mailing list is not appropriate, do not destroy your notes, but keep them, adding to them as you read through the archives of each mailing list to determine whether it is appropriate for your research. Later, share your experiences conducting research this way with other people in your class, learning from each other what worked and what did not work.

3. Find one person from one of your five mailing lists and one person from one of your five newsgroups to write to about your topic. Explain that you are writing to them as part of your class research project and that you would like to share their responses with others in your class. Using your best netiquette, ask them the question or questions that you would like more information about. Copy your e-mail inquiring about the topic and their responses. Share them with the class, discussing what worked and what did not work as research efforts.

FORUMS

Forums are places where individuals can create a discussion topic themselves or join in an existing discussion about a topic that someone else has already begun. They have the advantage over mail lists of allowing discussions to be structured and organized according to topics and subtopics, rather than the unstructured forms of mail lists. You have already learned how to use dejanews <http:www.dejanews.com> to search for newsgroups, so you should be pleased to learn that you can also use it to search for forums. A special forum finder at that site called *Interest Finder* allows you to locate a forum on you favorite topic. When you enter the topic you are looking for into the search box, *Interest Finder* returns a list of forums available on your topic.

OTHER RESEARCH TOOLS

After you become familiar with Web discussion tools such as e-mail, mailing lists, and newsgroups, consider exploring other Internet programs such as forums and MOOs. As the Web develops, new tools emerge. You should explore new kinds of communication tools that you read about, for some may be more valuable to your purposes than those you currently use.

Bruce Dobler and Harry Bloomberg, professors at the University of Pittsburgh, feel strongly that research projects that ignore the Internet are not acceptable pieces of work. They are particularly excited about the promise of UseNet, listserver discussion groups, and MOOs (explained below) for research.

> ... active on-line discussion in MOOs and various real-time chat rooms create an interactive research space. Documents that would have remained unpublished or published to very limited audiences are finding their way into worldwide distribution because the Web makes this practical for the first time. (68)

MOOs

Sometimes e-mail, mail lists, and forums can seem too formal, too structured. In addition, since those who send e-mail do not expect their addresses to be logged in at the moment and because readers indeed are not logged in all the time, a considerable amount of time can pass before someone responds to a message. Some people prefer technologies that allow them to write in real-time with other writers.

An unusual way to collaborate with research partners is by joining them in a MOO. MOO stands for MUD Object-Oriented, and MUD is an acronym for Multi-User Dungeon or, as many prefer, Multi-User Domain. These environments were created for game playing but have some potential for scholarship. One of the MOOs, MediaMOO, is used by media researchers at MIT and elsewhere. When you log in to MediaMOO, you are assigned a guest name (such as Purple Guest or Cyan Guest). If you are doing media research, you may be given the name of a character. Other MOOs, such as Diversity University and Daedalus MOO, allow students to work with other participants. It is difficult, of course, to coordinate schedules of people who live in different parts of the world, so meeting synchronously (at the same time) is not always easy. Typically, the participants arrange to meet at a given time by sending e-mail messages to one another first.

A MOO allows the creator to establish different areas where different participants can meet to discuss topics that they are interested in. A participant may move from one area to another and join different conversations in the different areas. Some MOOs, for example, organize these areas as though they are part of a building or a university campus. So one floor of a building may be devoted to a specific topic, and different rooms on that floor may be subtopics. Participants may agree to meet in a specific area of the MOO to discuss one topic one day and another topic another day. Each MOO will have its own rules and regulations, so as with mail lists, be sure to learn what the guidelines are before you plunge into the conversation.

One difficulty with MOOs is that the conversation may be among many different people at the same time. So if one participant responds to another participant about a specific topic of conversation, the original comment and the response may be separated by other comments to other participants because the comments appear as they arrive at the computer. To control for this, some groups of MOO participants agree to have one person serve as a moderator. But people who like MOOs like them because they allow participants to have immediate responses to whatever they write.

It is fairly simple to get connected to a MOO. If the MOO has a Web interface, you can access it by entering the http address into your browser's location box. If the MOO you want to reach has a Telnet address, then you will need to have a Telnet program installed on your computer. You can find educational MOOS at the following addresses:

Diversity University
telnet://moo.du.org:8888
(Note: This MOO is for diverse topics, not ethnic diversity per se.)

Virtual Online University
http://www.lac.net/~billp/
http://www.academic.marist.edu/duwww.htm

MOO Central
http://www.pitt.edu/~jrgst7/

MSCS–Educational MOOs
http://www.speakeasy.org/~pscs/moo.html

The Lost Library of MOO
http://lucien.sims.berkeley.edu/moo.html

PRACTICE BOX

1. Are you interested in conducting an informal survey for your research project? If so, post the survey to a mailing list dedicated to that topic. If you word your message carefully, you are likely to get some good results.

   Here is a sample survey: Ask the participants in a mailing list to indicate whether they use their e-mail program to categorize and sort data. If so, ask them to describe their techniques. Offer to post the results of your survey to the group. Be sure to design your survey so that e-mail respondents can complete it easily. Suggest that respondents include your message in their reply. In that way they can complete the survey online. Put items that can be checked with an *x* in the left-hand column so that they can be completed easily. When respondents return the survey, use e-mail folders to organize the responses. You might organize different types of respondents in different folders. Here's a sample of how you might format your e-mail survey:

   I sort notes in my e-mail folder:

   [ ] always

   [ ] sometimes

   [ ] never

   Save open-ended items for the end of the survey so that you can easily identify them.

2. Visit some of the following online writing labs (OWLs) and find out if they feature live MOO chat sessions: Purdue University <http://owl.trc.purdue.edu>, Bowling Green State University <http://www.bgsu.edu/departments/writing-lab/Homepage.html>, Michigan State University <http://www.hu.mtu.edu/~jdcolman/wc/welcome.html>, Rensselaer Polytechnical Institute <http://www.rpi.edu/dept/llc/writecenter/web/home.html>, University of Maine <http://www.ume.maine.edu/~wcenter>, and Dakota State University <http://www.dsu.edu/departments/liberal/owl/Dakota State>. Agree on a specific time and meet with others in your course or students at different schools who are interested in talking about the same topic.

3. Search for newsgroups and MOOs that would allow you and other members of the class to conduct research. Post the names, addresses, and purposes of the newsgroups and MOOs that you find, along with any hints you may have about using that particular newsgroup or MOO so that others can make use of your research into these sites.

CONCLUSION

You won't become an expert at using e-mail, mailing lists, newsgroups, and other tools for research while working on your first project; and you may wind up not citing any of the comments or ideas that you read. But just by listening in on the conversations about your topic, you are conducting exploratory research. If you do find information that you want to cite, consult the guidelines in Chapter 8 for documenting sources from e-mail, mailing lists, and newsgroups. Subscribe to a list related to your research interests. To find an appropriate mailing list, explore liszt—Directory of E-mail Discussion Groups <http://www.liszt.com/>.

EXERCISES

1. Join one or more newsgroups related to your topic. Follow the discussion for several weeks, taking notes on the ways people interact with one another. Note how new topics are introduced, how disagreements are managed, and how newcomers are treated. Examine messages to find evidence of shared understandings—beliefs or practices—that the writers have in common.

2. Discuss the validity of different messages. What makes one source better than another? Can you determine the credentials of the authors? If so, how?

3. Search the archives of the mailing list to which you are subscribed. What are the most typical topics that the e-mail authors have discussed? Which seem to generate the most responses? Why?

4. As you have researched newsgroups and mailing lists, you may have discovered some helpful hints for research. Write down some of the ideas that you have gathered for conducting research successfully.

5. Identify at least one expert whom you can interview online about your topic. Conduct the interview and incorporate it into your research.

6. *Optional*: Conduct a survey of your classmates on a topic related to your paper.

7 CHAPTER

Taking Notes and Organizing Information

After completing this chapter, you should be able to do the following:

■ Create bookmarks.

■ Organize and annotate bookmarks.

■ Set up an electronic workspace.

■ Create research directories.

■ Use a word processor to create electronic note cards.

■ Apply these techniques to your own research process.

In this chapter you will learn how to organize the sources of information you find so that you can access it as you are developing your research report, whether that information is from Web pages, newsgroups, mailing lists, or e-mail messages. You will first learn how to bookmark, or electronically tag, your sources so that you can call them up easily without having to search again. And you will learn how to organize those bookmarks so that they make some sort of logical sense to you as you begin drafting your report. Then you will learn how to organize your bookmarks on a disk so that you can take those bookmarks with you to another computer. Finally, the chapter summarizes how these procedures fit into the research process.

BOOKMARKING

As you are searching for sources of information, you will begin identifying particular Web sites that seem to be worth saving or returning to so that you can use the information at the sites for your research project. You can save yourself a great deal of time in the future by **bookmarking** the site. When you bookmark a site, you electronically tag it with the electronic address of the site and a name for the site. Each Web browser (such as Netscape or Microsoft Explorer enables bookmarking through slightly different, though similar, means, so you should learn how to bookmark files for your particular browser.

When you have located a Web site with valuable information for your research and while the site is still online, go to your bookmark menu and choose **Add Bookmarks**. The site you have identified will automatically be added to a bookmark list. Then, whenever you are online, you can go to your bookmark list, click on the bookmark that you want, and your browser will take you to that site. Note that the bookmark is actually saved on the hard disk of your computer, not online anywhere, so you will only be able to access the bookmarks online from this computer, unless you save your bookmarks on a disk as described later in this chapter.

PRACTICE BOX

Go to the Web and start searching for a topic that interests you. When you find a Web site that you want to go back to sometime, go to the **bookmark** area of your Web browser and click on **add bookmark**. Your bookmark is now saved on the hard disk of your computer. To view your bookmark, simply return to the bookmark area, and you will see your bookmark title displayed. Click on it, and you will be back to your Web site.

As you add bookmarks, each bookmark will be added to the bottom of the list of bookmarks. When you are first starting to work with bookmarks, this is an adequate way to store your bookmarks. However, as you find more and more sites to bookmark, you will want to organize your bookmarks so that you can quickly find the particular sites you want. This is especially important because, while you might begin storing bookmarks for your paper on marketing automobiles, air supply strategies, or affirmative action, if you are like most people, you will be discovering other sites that relate to your personal interests, hobbies, and projects that you work on when you are not preparing your research report. Naturally, you will want to bookmark those as well. Soon, you will discover that your bookmarks are all mixed together and increasingly difficult to identify unless you develop a strategy for organizing them.

Organizing Bookmarks

In this section, you will learn how to create bookmarks—electronic addresses that enable you to go rapidly to Web sites that are valuable to you, how to annotate the bookmarks, and how to collect the bookmarks in folders so that you have collections of bookmarks that relate to one another. By being able to use these techniques, you will make your use of the Web efficient and effective.

Creating Bookmark Files

The first thing you probably want to do is to collect your bookmarks in different files for different purposes. For example, if you are working on a research paper, you will want to have a bookmark file for you research project. When you have a collection of bookmarks all related to the topic of your research project, you can go to your file menu and save the entire list of bookmarks as a bookmark file by simply selecting the **save as** command and giving your list whatever name you want so that you can identify it and come back to it later. You can save as many bookmark files as you want to keep collections related to other bookmark topics, such as hobbies or other research projects or other special interests. Figure 7.1 below shows just such a "master collection" of bookmark files. Notice that it contains personal interest folders, folders with key research sources, and a folder related to the research project on affirmative action.

Creating Folders

Within your collection of bookmarks, or bookmark file, you can organize your bookmarks by first creating *folders* and then filing your bookmarks in these

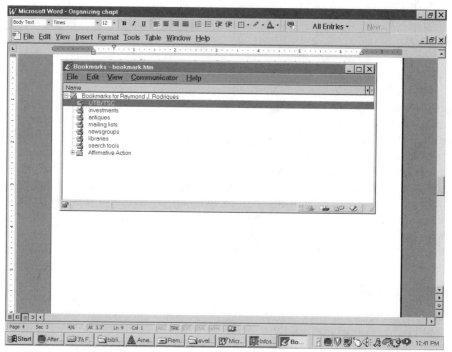

FIGURE 7.1   Example of a personal set of bookmark folders.

folders. You can create a folder by going to the bookmark section of your browser and clicking on the area that allows you to add a folder. When you do this, you will be asked to give the folder a name. Name your folders with a more general name than the specific title of the bookmarked Web site or sites within that folder. Before you find all the sites you want to bookmark for your research topic, you might even brainstorm a set of other folders that might relate to your research topic and create those folders before you have bookmarks to fill them. See Figure 7.2 for an example of a bookmark file with brainstormed folders that might be appropriate for a research paper on affirmative action.

Notice that in Figure 7.2 the bookmark file is not only organized according to folders but also subfolders. You can create as many folders as you want as you gather more and more bookmarks. You can also move your bookmarks around from folder to folder by clicking and dragging the name of the bookmark or by clicking and dragging the folder to where you want to reposition it. You will find that, as you begin to develop new folders and subfolders of bookmarks related to your research project, you also will be helping yourself to think of ways you may want to organize your research report. In this early stage of your research, be as creative as you want to be, for adding and deleting folders and subfolders is easy once you learn how to do it.

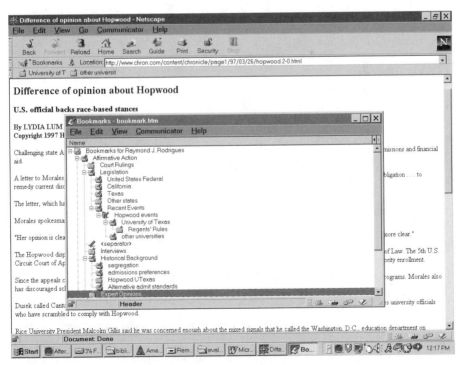

FIGURE 7.2 Example of a set of brainstormed bookmark folders and subfolders at the early stage of collecting and bookmarking possible sources for a research project.

PRACTICE BOX

1. After you have collected several bookmarks on any topics you want, save a bookmark file with a title that you give it. Then collect more bookmarks and save them in a different bookmark file. Practice moving from one bookmark file to another.

2. Now select a topic that you think you would like to write your research paper on. Begin collecting bookmarks related to that topic and save them in a bookmark file titled, e.g., Research Paper, or whatever title you want to give it so that you can identify it.

3. After you have collected several sites related to your research paper and read through those sites, begin thinking of the various topics that might be possible within your future paper. Create folders for each of those topics. If you happen to think of subtopics, create subfolders for them. If you have difficulty thinking of many topics, sit down with a friend or classmate and help each other think of subtopics for your papers by brainstorming together or by asking each other questions about your topics.

4. Practice moving folders and subfolders around within your research paper bookmark file. Sometimes this helps you think of different ways to organize the paper that you have yet to write and also helps you think of possible Web site topics to search for in doing your early research on the Web.

Figure 7.3 indicates what a Netscape screen looks like as the researcher files a new bookmark file in a subfolder within a subfolder within a folder.

Annotating Bookmarks

In addition to collecting bookmarks and placing them in bookmark files and folders within bookmark files, try to get in the habit of routinely annotating— or describing with brief notes—those bookmark sites. While you might easily remember the purpose of the bookmarks you save when you first start saving them, after a while you may have a great number of bookmarked sites, many with similar or almost identical titles. It is very time-consuming if you have to go to each one to determine what they are about, but by jotting down a brief description and reaction to each site, your bookmark collection becomes a set of electronic note cards. The annotations remind you of the content as well as the merit of each site.

To annotate a source, select **edit** from the bookmark menu, and then the **preferences** section of the menu, which should lead you to a screen where you can write a brief description of your bookmark. Type a summary of what is in the source within the description section of the screen. Figure 7.4, on page 94, shows you a sample of a bookmark file that has been annotated. Note all that

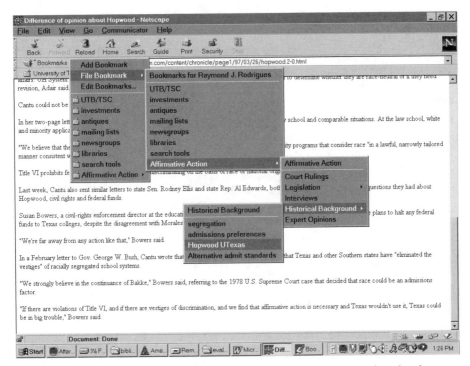

FIGURE 7.3 Examples of subfolders within subfolders as the researcher develops categories for filing bookmarks.

is automatically included in the Bookmark Properties box: the title of the original source, the URL, even the time and date when the bookmark was added to the list of bookmarks.

Note also that the researcher's description of the source first states what is in the source and then adds a note that indicates the source may now be historical in nature and may not reflect the latest developments on the topic.

If you are creating bookmarks and organizing them into folders on a computer in a computer lab at your college or on some other public computer, you should not leave those bookmarks on that computer, for someone else may

PRACTICE BOX

1. Along with each other person in this class, practice annotating one Web site source. Contrast the ways that each person annotates the source. Develop a set of guidelines for good annotations.
2. Begin annotating the bookmarks that you have already collected.

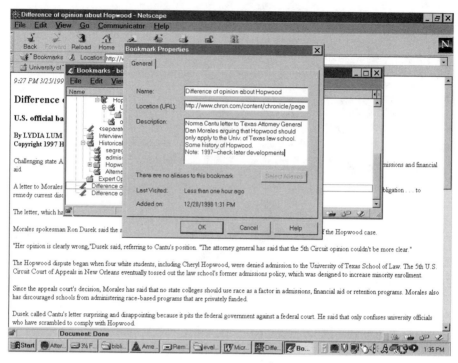

FIGURE 7.4 Example of an annotation for a bookmark.

erase them. Remember that the bookmarks are saved on your computer's hard drive. Therefore, if you save your files on a computer disk, you can take your disk with its bookmarks home or to another computer in the lab to work on it when you next have time. To save your bookmark file to a disk, you go to the bookmark menu, go to the **save as** line, and save it to the appropriate disk drive. For example, you might type in "a:research topic," and the computer will save your bookmark file to the *a* drive.

Your bookmarks are automatically saved as an HTML file every time you exit your browser. Netscape automatically names the file in a way that it recognizes as a bookmark file. But remember you are not saving the text or pictures of the Web sites that you have bookmarked. You are only saving the Web addresses, so if you want to have separate notes or quotes from those Web sites, you will have to save them into word processing files.

SETTING UP YOUR ELECTRONIC WORK SPACE

Whether you will be working on your own computer at home or working on a computer in a computer lab and therefore saving everything to a computer disk, you will want to create files for various parts of your research process. Take time to organize an effective workspace either on your home computer's hard drive or on a computer disk that you can move from computer to computer or both. You will do this either by establishing your own *file structures* with the word processing program or through a separate *utility program*. When you use the **save as** command, you can create directories and subdirectories in which to save your files. Even if you do not have your own computer, try to think through ways of organizing your files into folders on a disk. Use that disk or set of disks exclusively for your research project. Although you will probably want to refine the techniques in this section to suit your own work style, some version of it may be useful to you.

Here are the kinds of files and directories to consider establishing:

1. A directory for your research project.
2. A *research notebook* directory or file where you keep notes to yourself about your research and ideas for how to organize your research.
3. A set of subdirectories or files where you write notes or copy pertinent quotes from the Web sites that you may use in your research project. (In most cases, you won't think of these until after your research is underway. So simply create them as you realize that they will be helpful to you later.)
4. A directory or file that serves as a combination *note card* and *bibliography card* file—with template note cards that you use to take notes from your sources (either typing in notes or pasting in portions of online sources).
5. A directory for drafts of your research paper, with each draft saved as a separate file (e.g., Audit Guidelines 1, Audit Guidelines 2, and so on).

Figure 7.5 shows an example of how you can organize your electronic workspace.

THE RESEARCH PROJECT DIRECTORY

The research project directory holds subdirectories for all your work related to a designated research project, including e-mail notes and bibliographic entries, your research notebook, and the drafts of your research paper itself. If you are saving everything to a computer disk, you might prefer to dedicate the entire disk to the sole purpose of the research paper. (Note: If they have to work on different computers, some people have two separate copies on separate disks in case one is lost or accidentally destroyed.)

Research Notebook Directory

The research notebook directory or file (see Figure 7.6) will help you write reminders to yourself. For example, while browsing a particular Web site, you might find a reference to a particular print source that you want to search for in your library, one that is not online, so you write a note with the title, author,

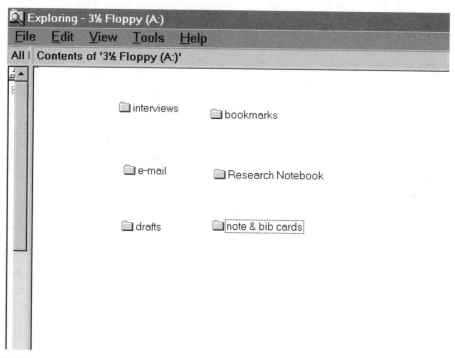

FIGURE 7.5   Example of an electronic workspace.

and whatever other bibliographic information you need to find that possible source. Or you think of a new subtopic to explore, but you don't have the time to do so at the moment. Or you find a better source or quote than one that you had already included in a draft of your paper, and you want to remember to substitute this new one.

Your research notebook might also include a chart in which you evaluate your sources. Here is a sample of what such a chart might look like:

SOURCE	LIBRARY LOCATION	INTERNET LOCATION	VALUE OF SOURCE * Promising ** Good *** Excellent
Difference of opinion about Hopwood		www.chron.com/content/ chronicle/page	**newspaper article different opinions

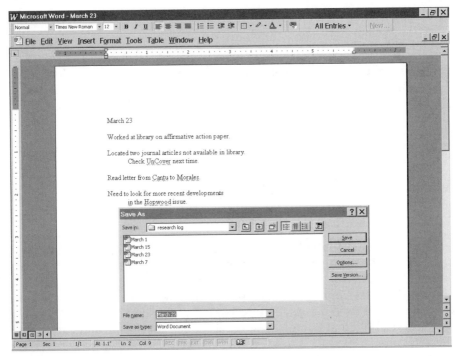

FIGURE 7.6 Example of a research notebook directory (a log kept as the research proceeds).

Subtopic Directories

Subtopic directories serve many purposes. Somes files in the subtopic directory might be Web pages that have served as a unit. Other files might contain e-mail messages or quotes copied and pasted into the subdirectory from newsgroups or mailing lists. (Be sure that you note the source of whatever you copy in case you use it in your research paper, for you will need to cite it; and you may want to return to the full source at a later date.) Still another file may be a collection of note cards on this topic that you have copied from your research notebook or note cards that you have written in the library using various print sources for your research paper. If you include subdirectories and files for your research notes and the drafts of your papers, you can easily move from one file to another.

Electronic Note Cards

Create an electronic note card file for note taking. Design a template, or form, to use in your note card file. After you design your note card, copy it about ten times so that you have a set of blank template note cards.

To design a master template file, follow these steps:

1. Open a new file with your word processor.
2. Type the categories you want to use. Do not fill them in.
3. Save the file with an identifiable name, such as "bib.temp" for bibliographic template.

To use the template file:

1. Load the master template file (e.g., bib.temp).
2. Use the **Save as** feature of your word processor to give the file a new name (e.g., "literature.bib").
   Note: Be sure to rename this file each time you create it, or else you will overwrite the master file. If you create separate copies at different times, be sure to name them differently from the earlier files you have written into (e.g., "literature2.bib").

If you design your bibliography cards to match the way your library presents the results of library searches, then you can copy and paste your library search results directly onto your bibliography file.

Consider developing a system for note taking. In the example in Figure 7.7, the student used a script font to indicate notes that he took in his own words and a bold font to indicate snippets of text that he cut and pasted into the note card.

Even though you may not decide to quote portions of text that you place on your note card, the ease of copying and pasting makes it possible to have

PRACTICE BOX

1. Since each word processing program is slightly different, develop a way of organizing files, folders, and directories that will work for your program. How do you insert an existing file into a file you are using? Be ready to share your strategy and technical solutions with others who may use the same word processing package.

2. Practice capturing your library searches to a file so that you can incorporate the results into note card and bibliography card files.

3. Practice capturing portions of your Web searches into your electronic note card and bibliography card files. Be sure to include the bibliographic information you need to cite the sources if you use this information in your research paper.

4. Develop an alternative way of organizing your electronic work area and share it with others.

Author: Bradley, Bill

Title: Ending Racism Can Never Be Just about Numbers

Published: Los Angeles Times, Monday, January 15, 1996
    Home Edition   Metro, Page 5

Description: Opinion, transcript

Notes: *This is from a speech Bradley gave. Bradley feels that the issue is discrimination and that it has been that since the 60s. The assumption is that, if we could get rid of racism, we could have a* "spiritually transformed America."

Bradley says that instead of talking about getting rid of affirmative action, we should focus on getting people from all racial backgrounds to interact more with one another: "A new political vision requires people to engage each other, endure the pain, learn from each other's history, absorb each other's humanity and move on to higher ground. It won't happen overnight, nor will one person bring it about, however illustrative his career; nor will one person destroy it, however heinous his crime or poisonous his rhetoric."

Subjects: Racism

Author: Slater, Robert Bruce

Title: Why Socioeconomic Affirmative Action in College Admission Works against African Americans

Published: Journal of Blacks in Higher Education, The, 06-30-1995, pp. PG.

Description:

Notes: *The author notes that the number of blacks at many schools would go down dramatically if socioeconomic status were used instead of race and ethnicity.*
"First, they found that if all selections were based on academic standing and standardized test scores alone, the percentage of blacks in the freshman class would drop from 6 percent to between 0.5 percent and 1.9 percent. White enrollment would rise by as much as 25 percent from its present level of 29.8 percent of Berkeley's freshman class. Asian enrollment, which was 41.7 percent of the 1994 entering freshman class . . ."

FIGURE 7.7 Sample electronic bibliography card/note card file with student's notes in script and quoted in boldface.

exact words of an author easily at your disposal. As long as you are careful to avoid plagiarism, you should use the power that technology affords you.

Sometimes you will want to type directly into your template file. Other times you will copy into your file portions of text from Web sites that you are considering quoting and citing.

If you have saved Web pages to separate files, you may wish to open the Web page in one window of your word processor and your note card or bibliography card in another, so that you can take notes or cut and paste, switching from the text of your Web file to your note card and back.

Draft Files

Open a separate file to draft your paper. If you keep your note cards file (and selected subtopic files) open as you draft, you can move files as you write. Many authors also create an outline file to guide them as they work.

When you are ready to revise your files, make a new copy of the last draft that you wrote, and revise it rather than revising the original file. This uses up more space on your computer disk or your hard drive, but you may decide later that you deleted something that you now wish you had not deleted. By keeping all the earlier drafts, you can always go into them to retrieve something for a later file.

Finally, do not start writing your research paper until you have had a chance to read many sources related to your topic. You need to understand as much about the topic as you can before you decide upon the specific focus of your topic or thesis for your paper. The more you read (and take notes) first, the more likely you are to pick a topic that both interests you and that provides you with a topic that is worth writing about.

E-MAIL AS AN ORGANIZATIONAL TOOL

Take time to learn how to organize your e-mail into folders that correspond to the folders you are using to take notes from library and Web sources. Each e-mail program is difficult, so you will have to learn how to use the program on your personal computer or, if you are using a computer at work or school, you will need to learn how to organize your e-mail folders on a disk. Do not make the mistake of leaving all of your messages in your inbox. Eventually, your inbox will fill up, and if you are not careful, it may cause your computer to crash.

Most browsers, including Netscape, allow you to send the text of the page you are viewing to your e-mail address. This is particularly handy if you are in the library or computer lab using a Web browser. If you use e-mail from within Netscape, you can attach any Web page to an e-mail message, send the page to yourself, and then retrieve the message at your own computer. When you retrieve the file, be sure to save it to an appropriate subdirectory.

SUMMARIZING THE ORGANIZATIONAL PROCESS

1. Begin browsing through the Web and through your library online to locate possible sources to include in your research project. Use search engines to narrow the possible specific sites on various aspects of your topic. Do not restrict your topic too much when you start.

PRACTICE BOX

1. How do you save to different folders in your e-mail program? Learn the steps and write them inside the back cover of this book.
2. Create several folders in your e-mail program. How do you move the notes in these folders to a directory in your word processor? Write that inside the back cover of this book.
3. Locate a source on the Web and copy part of it to a computer disk. Be sure to copy the bibliographic data as well.
4. Review the way you organized your bookmarks in preparation for your research. Do you need to reorganize them now that you have learned and thought more about your research topic? If so, do so.
5. Review your directories and subdirectories in your electronic workspace. Consider reorganizing them in preparation for writing your first draft of your research paper.
6. Study your electronic note and bibliography cards. Put them in the order you intend to use them while writing your first draft of your research paper.

2. Bookmark your sources as you locate them by using the **Add Bookmark** command of your browser. Add as many as you want: they do not take up much space, and you can always delete them later.
3. Annotate your bookmarks so that you can remember what they were about and how useful they might be.
4. As your bookmark file starts to grow, and as soon as you have a sense of the categories into which you might sort your sources, organize your research project bookmark file into folders and subfolders. Put your bookmarks into the folder or subfolder where you think they belong.
5. Organize your electronic workspace (whether on the hard drive of your computer or a computer disk) into directories and subdirectories, including a research notebook, electronic note or bibliography card area, bookmark file area, and other areas that you might find useful as you conduct your research, such as directories for interviews, newsgroups, or mailing lists.
6. Make electronic note and bibliography cards on the sources you intend to use so that you can quote and/or cite your sources accurately.
7. Begin drafting your research paper when you have read enough to understand your subject well. Move back and forth between your notes and the draft, cutting and pasting from your other file as appropriate.
8. For each subsequent revision of your draft, create a new word processing file.

CONCLUSION

Systematic strategies for finding, capturing, and organizing information from the Web enable you to make your computer a major research tool. As you are developing your research topic, you should be thinking of various ways of organizing the information you find so that you can later pull it together into a meaningfully organized research paper. The computer allows you to establish the categories you want and store information in those categories, but it also allows you to reorganize those categories later if you develop new ways of conceptualizing and presenting the research that you find.

The same points may be made as you begin writing your research paper. You should consider each version of the paper as a draft that can be revised and reorganized. You will begin to think of the Web and your computer as tools that enable you to reorganize information, reconceptualize topics and subtopics, and focus on your points more clearly. This will enable you to write a more effective research paper, and your ability to continuously improve your research paper will gradually develop.

EXERCISES

1. Review the sources for your paper that you have identified to date. Discard those that you no longer need.

2. Bookmark sources on the Web by using the **Add Bookmark** feature of your browser. Add as many as you want. They do not take up space, for all you are doing is adding a link to the URL for each site.

3. Annotate your bookmarks so that you can remember what they were about and how useful they might be.

4. As your bookmark file starts to grow and as soon as you have a sense of the categories into which you might sort your resources, organize your research project bookmark file into folders and subfolders. Put your bookmarks into the most logical folder or subfolder.

5. Organize your electronic workspace (whether on the hard drive of your computer or on a computer disk) into directories and subdirectories, including a research notebook, electronic note card and bibliography card area, bookmark file area, and other areas that you might find useful.

6. Make electronic note and bibliography cards on the sources you intend to use so that you can quote and/or cite from them accurately.

7. Begin drafting your research paper when you have read enough to understand your subject well. Move back and forth between your notes and the draft, cutting and pasting from your files as appropriate.

8. For each subsequent revision of your draft, create a new word processing file.

CHAPTER 8

Documenting Sources

After completing this chapter, you should be able to do the following:

■ Learn how to summarize sources.

■ Learn how to paraphrase sources.

■ Know how to quote from sources and integrate them into your draft.

■ Know when to cite from sources.

■ Determine the appropriate citation style for your research paper.

■ Apply correct citation practices to your own sources.

■ Whenever guidelines do not specify the style for a type of source you have located, be able to adapt existing citation models to the source.

Your readers should be able to understand how your sources support your line of argument or your interpretation of evidence. The readers should also be able to locate the sources themselves if they want to learn more from them or if they want to judge the reliability of sources themselves.

When you write your research paper, you let your readers know where you found your information by documenting your sources. The term *documenting sources* refers to the process of keeping track of your information and citing it properly in your completed research report. This chapter discusses whether to summarize, paraphrase, or quote a source; reviews the basics of documentation style; provides you with a sample paper; and then turns to Internet and Web citation styles.

DIFFERENT CITATION STYLES IN DIFFERENT DISCIPLINES

Specialists in disciplines such as English or Sociology or Business Administration have worked over the years to establish conventions for citing sources in their respective disciplines. While they all have a common purpose, the styles differ somewhat, so when you are writing a research paper for a course, you should find out what documentation style your professor wants you to use. This chapter covers the Modern Language Association (MLA) style, which is used in the humanities, and the American Psychological Association (APA) style, which is most often used in the social sciences and business. Other fields, such as the sciences and mathematics, use different style guides. Check the Web site for this chapter for information on using style guides in other fields of study.

You may think it would make more sense if all disciplines simply followed the same guidelines. Perhaps, but there are reasons why different disciplines prefer different citation styles. Scholars in the social sciences, for example, are more interested in the date a work was published than are scholars in the humanities. Thus, a standard reference to a book in MLA style refers to the author and page number in the internal citation (e.g., Rodrigues 36) whereas a similar citation in APA style for a social science or science report would provide the date (e.g., Rodrigues 1996).

Here, briefly, is an overview of the two documentation styles covered in this book: MLA style calls for a source name and a page reference for internal (in-text) citations, which refers a reader to a Works Cited list at the end of the paper for more complete information. APA style calls for a source name and year (and, if you have an exact quote, a page reference for in-text citations), which refers the reader to the References list at the end of the paper.

The style and format for the research paper itself varies from one discipline to the next. Humanities research papers tend to be written in a style whose structure is not very overt, whereas social sciences and science papers use a more formal report format with specified headings and subheadings. Check with your instructor for specific guidelines.

SUMMARIZING, PARAPHRASING, AND QUOTING

As a researcher, you will need to use information or ideas that others have developed or written themselves, and so you will need to decide how best to incorporate that information or those ideas into your own writing. You have three choices available: to summarize, to paraphrase, or to quote. And whichever you choose, you must cite the sources to be honest as a scholar.

Summarizing

A summary is a short, concise version of the main idea or ideas of your source. Summarize when you want to refer to the general idea of what you have read, but do not want to go into all the detail or use all of the words in the original. It may be, for example, that the writer has so many details that it would only confuse or bore your reader to include them all. So you summarize the essence of those details. It may be that the writer's style is not particularly memorable or different from what others have written on the subject, so quoting would not make sense.

Sometimes you read several sources that are all making the same point. In this case, it would make sense to summarize all of them together and cite them as a group (e.g., Bradley 1996, Roser 1998, Smith 1999).

When you summarize, use your own words, leave out specific details and facts, and be brief. Do not add your own interpretation to the summary. It is acceptable to add your own interpretation before or after the summary, but not as part of it. Respect the original author's ideas and efforts.

Original

As a child in the 1950s, Clarence Thomas wore the ragged hand-me-downs familiar to many a poor black child in the segregated South. In the early 1960s, as the first black ever enrolled at St. John Vianney Minor Seminary, in Savannah, Georgia, he wore plain, neatly pressed shirts and slacks, along with an expression that bespoke a painful shyness. . . .

Now thirty-eight, and the chairman of the U.S. Equal Employment Opportunity Commission (EEOC), Clarence Thomas dresses in dark, elegant, conservative business suits. He earns $71,000 a year and, when he is not being chauffeured in a government car, drives a Camaro IROC-Z. Behind his leather chair stand two flags, one the Stars and Stripes and the other bearing the legend "Don't Tread on Me." It is an apt motto for the head of an agency charged with ensuring that discrimination based on race, sex, age, religion, or national origin does not occur in the workplace, and that should it occur, appropriate steps are taken to seek redress. (From an article by Juan Williams in the May 1, 1999, *Atlantic Monthly*, contained in the online version at <http://www.theatlantic.com/unbound/flashbks/affact/thomasf.htm>.)

Summary of article. This article provides background on Clarence Thomas that helps readers understand his opposition to affirmative action because of the way it helps those already destined for success while at the same time reinforcing racial stereotypes.

Observation

The summary doesn't go into detail; it puts the main idea into a few sentences. If you summarize your sources this way, you are much more likely to remember what you have read, for your notes will emphasize the importance of your sources.

Paraphrasing

When you paraphrase, you put the original idea in your own words. Paraphrase when you want to include the ideas or facts of the original, but you want to put it in your own style or make it fit the context of what you are writing about at the time. Paraphrases usually are about the same length of the original, for they are capturing more than a summary does.

Paraphrase as a way of avoiding too many quotations in your paper. Paraphrase when the original meaning is what you want to capture, not necessarily the way the original is written. Paraphrase when you want to use details from the original, but not necessarily all of them and not necessarily in the same order as the original. Paraphrase and summarize when the original quote would be too long for your research paper.

There is a danger in paraphrasing, though: if you are not careful, you may be using the original writer's words or ideas or facts in such a way that you are actually quoting. If you cannot say something better than the original writer said it, then you probably should quote rather than paraphrase. And if you must quote some words in the paraphrase, then do so, but put them in quotation marks so that the reader knows this was not your wording.

Original

UT is appealing the Hopwood ruling, but arguments to the 5th U.S. Circuit Court of Appeals probably won't be scheduled until next spring or summer. And if the case goes to the U.S. Supreme Court, it could be 2000 or 2001 before the issue of racial considerations in higher education is resolved, said Betty Owens, an attorney for Vinson & Elkins, which is representing the UT case.

Owens appeared at one of two panel discussions Wednesday afternoon that drew about 75 students and explored racism, access to higher education and the fate of affirmative action. (From an article by Mary Ann Roser in the October 22, 1998, *Austin American Statesman*, contained in the online version at <http://austin360.com:80/news/features/hopwood/9810/22racism.htm>.)

Paraphrase. Even though the University of Texas decided to appeal the Hopwood ruling, an attorney working for the firm that is representing the University indicated that it would be two or three years before the case could actually be on the Supreme Court's agenda.

Observation

Since this information is being included in a paper on affirmative action as timely information about the arguments surrounding the Fifth Circuit Court of Appeals' Hopwood decision to limit affirmative action in admissions to the law school at the University of Texas, the writer uses the original material to indicate that a legal decision takes time. Quoting the original is not necessary;

a summary would be appropriate for the entire original article, not for the limited information referred to here.

Quoting

A quote is an exact use of the original writer's words and is indicated by the use of quotation marks before and after the quoted words. Use quotes when a writer says something so well that you could not possibly capture the idea as well by paraphrasing or summarizing. Quote when your paraphrase would end up being longer or more confusing than the original quote. Quote when the original words carry with them some importance that helps make a point, such as when the writer is an absolute authority on the subject or when the writer is so well known that your reader will understand the importance of that person's words.

Do not, however, fill your research report with quote after quote. If you do, your reader is liable to conclude that you really have no ideas of your own on the subject or that you have not studied and understood the subject well enough to begin to form your own opinions. It seems as though you are saying, "Here's one person's ideas on the subject and here's another's and here's another's and . . . "

Before you include the quote, you should indicate something about it so that your reader understands why you are quoting and the context of the quote within your total paper. As another stylistic choice, it may be easier for the reader to understand the purpose for the quote if you briefly introduce the quote and then comment on it.

Original

In trying to summarize the dilemma that policymakers are faced with when confronted with having to provide equity for everyone in admitting students to college, the President of the University of Texas at Austin, Larry Faulkner, said, "If we could find methods that are as effective and do not depend on race-based decision-making, we would be better off as a society. . . . The question is whether there are other methods." (From an article written by Mary Ann Roser in the online version of the *Austin American Statesman*, October 24, 1998 <http://austin.360.com:80/news/features/hopwood/9810/24utrace.htm>.)

Observation

Note that the writer of the research paper has led into the quote by placing it within the context of the varying arguments regarding race-based admission standards. The writer also establishes the paper's perspective that the issue is a dilemma, a problem with no perfect solution. Then the quote itself encapsulates that dilemma well, thereby justifying its being quoted.

PRACTICE BOX

1. Decide whether to summarize, paraphrase, or quote the following quotations. Explain your choices:

   a. "Well, I do not think that you should restrict someone from learning more than one language. In fact, people make a living as translators by knowing more than English. It's an advantage to anyone because he or she will have more knowledge and will be one step ahead of the others." (From a student interview for a paper on the English-only legislation.)

   b. "McGwire and Sosa gave America a summer than won't be forgotten: a summer of stroke and counterstroke, of packed houses and curtain calls, of rivals embracing and gloves in the bleachers and adults turned into kids—the Summer of Long Balls and Love. . . . Never have two men chased legends and each other that hard and that long or invited so much of America onto their backs for the ride." (From an introduction by Gary Smith to articles on Mark McGwire and Sammy Sosa in the December 21, 1998, *Sports Illustrated*, p. 42.)

   c. "Although the Dow Jones Industrial Average and the S&P 500 made new highs in November, the broader market measures, such as the Wilshire 5000, fell well short. To bears, this was ominously reminiscent of the Nifty Fifty period in 1972–73. Then, blue-chip strength temporarily masked a market massacre that began much earlier in the secondary stocks—and preceded a serious recession. (From an article by Peter Brimelow in the December 28, 1998, *Forbes*, pp. 72–78, explaining different experts' perceptions about the immediate future of the stock market.)

2. Go back in this book and find one example of each section that you would summarize, a section that you would paraphrase, and a section that you would quote if you were doing a paper on how to do research on the Web. Share your selections with your classmates and be prepared to explain each of your choices.

WHAT TO CITE? AVOIDING PLAGIARISM

If you use someone's words without giving that person credit, you are guilty of plagiarism. Even if you have accidentally omitted a citation to a source, your instructor or employer may think that you have intentionally plagiarized. Your instructor has no way to differentiate between the two. Be careful also to cite sources that are not "common knowledge." As a rule of thumb, ask,

"Are other students in class or employees at work likely to have known this before they read my paper?" If the answer is no, then you should include a citation for your source.

At times, however, you may find yourself in the position of having learned so much about your source, that what you say is common knowledge to anyone who has read in depth on the topic. For example, if you are researching the Clinton impeachment case, you may be able to define the term *impeachment* without citing a specific source. In that case, you just define the topic in your own words. You are not guilty of plagiarism.

INTERNAL CITATION AND BIBLIOGRAPHIC CITATION

To properly document a research paper, you must use two types of citations: internal citations within the body of your paper and bibliographic citations listed at the end of your paper.

Internal, or in-text, citations in parentheses provide the key publication information about sources you have used. The purpose of a parenthetical in-text citation is to acknowledge the information source and to refer the reader to the list of bibliographic citations at the end of your paper. The bibliographic citations, arranged into a list alphabetized by author names, provide all of the pertinent publication information about the sources referred to in internal citations. This list is given different names in different documentation styles: in MLA it is called Works Cited, while in APA it is called References.

Here are some important aspects of in-text citation, which replaces the outmoded style of using footnotes at the bottoms of pages:

1. If you refer to the author in your sentence, do not repeat the author's name in the parentheses.

MLA: In the *Research Paper and the World Wide Web,* Rodrigues discusses ways to link Internet research and standard library research.

APA: In *The Research Paper and the World Wide Web* (1997), Rodrigues discusses ways to link Internet research and standard library research.

2. If you do not refer to the author's name in your sentence, then you must include the author's name in parentheses.

> **MLA:** In the *Research Paper and the World Wide Web*, the author discusses ways to link Internet research and standard library research (Rodrigues).

> **APA:** The *Research Paper and the World Wide Web* (Rodrigues, 1997) presents ways to link Internet research and standard library research.

Guidelines for Internal Citations

Documentation should be used sparingly and skillfully. Don't just collect a disorganized array of sources and quote them at random. Instead, organize the points you want to make and then refer to your sources by integrating them into the flow of your argument. Remember to use "tag" lines such as the following:

■ As the author notes . . .
■ Another author disagrees. Harris says that [paraphrase of source] . . .
■ In her book on [subject], Rodrigues writes . . .

Consider the following ways the author of the MLA paper, included later in this chapter, has incorporated sources and how the sources would be cited in APA style:

1. Paraphrasing an Indirect Source

> **MLA:** President Lyndon Johnson issued Executive Order 11246 calling for "affirmative action" among federal contractors, colleges, universities, and the federal government. The intent of this order was to increase the numbers of minorities and women in colleges, universities, and federal programs (qtd. in Lappe, 89).

APA: President Lyndon Johnson issued Executive Order 11246 calling for "affirmative action" among federal contractors, colleges, universities, and the federal government. The intent of this order was to increase the numbers of minorities and women in colleges, universities, and federal programs (qtd. in Lappe, 1989).

2. Using a Block Quotation

MLA: He explained the need for affirmative action in a June 1965 address at Howard University, noting that freedom of opportunity doesn't immediately level the playing field.

> You do not take a man who for years has been hobbled by chains, liberate him, bring him to the starting line of a race, saying "you are free to compete with all others," and still justly believe you have been completely fair. Thus it is not enough to open the gates of opportunity (qtd. in Lappe, 89).

APA: He explained the need for affirmative action in a June 1965 address at Howard University, noting that freedom of opportunity doesn't immediately level the playing field.

> You do not take a man who for years has been hobbled by chains, liberate him, bring him to the starting line of a race, saying "you are free to compete with all others," and still justly believe you have been completely fair. Thus it is not enough to open the gates of opportunity (qtd. in Lappe, 1995, p. 89).

3. Quoting a Complete Sentence from a Source

MLA: As Pedro Noguera points out, "Without a policy that holds universities and employers accountable for who they admit, the pledge to not discriminate is meaningless" (50).

APA: As Pedro Noguera (1996) points out, "Without a policy that holds universities and employers accountable for who they admit, the pledge to not discriminate is meaningless" (p. 50).

4. Identifying the Origin of a Source without Quoting It

MLA: **A study done found that students from all racial and ethnic groups showed strong support for diversity efforts in the curriculum (Lopez, 33).**

APA: A study found that students from all racial and ethnic groups showed strong support for diversity efforts in the curriculum (Lopez, 1995).

5. Quoting Only a Few Words from a Source

MLA: **Some groups argue that affirmative action isn't really needed in some parts of the country. One group of students at the University of California (Students Against Affirmative Action and for Equality) has argued that diversity would exist on their campus without what they see as offensive "racially based guidelines," since they live in a place with a mix of cultures (Greenman).**

APA: Some groups argue that affirmative action isn't really needed in some parts of the country. One group of students at the University of California (Students Against Affirmative Action and for Equality) has argued that diversity would exist on their campus without what they see as offensive "racially based guidelines," since they live in a place with a mix of cultures (Greenman, 1996).

6. Quoting a Portion of a Sentence

MLA: Columnist Bill Bradley is convinced that racism and discrimination won't go away easily because "many people hold values that allow them to defend the social advantage they have based on being upper class whites" (10).

APA: Columnist Bill Bradley (1996) is convinced that racism and discrimination won't go away easily because "many people hold values that allow them to defend the social advantage they have based on being upper class whites" (p. 10).

7. Introducing a Source with "Tag" Words (Such as "As X argues")

MLA: As R. Richard Banks argues, there is an increasing reluctance of intellectuals and politicians to identify social problems as explicitly racial problems (45).

APA: As R. Richard Banks (1995) argues, there is an increasing reluctance of intellectuals and politicians to identify social problems as explicitly racial problems.

8. Summarizing an Entire Source

MLA: Richard Kalenberg offers a choice of several ways to address class rather than race in college admissions, ranging from a simple reporting of family income to a more complex series of calculations based on factors such as the neighborhood where a student lives, the quality of the high school that he or she may have attended, and family income.

APA: Richard Kalenberg (1995) offers a choice of several ways to address class rather than race in college admissions, ranging from a simple reporting of family income to a more complex series of calculations based on factors such as the neighborhood where a student lives, the quality of the high school that he or she may have attended, and family income.

9. Using a Combination of Methods

MLA: Banks feels that both race and class have to be factored in, even though race matters more. In "Race Matters More," he maintains that proposals to base affirmative action on economic class alone rather than on race ignore fundamental truths about the interplay of race and class (32). Banks feels that if we really cared about helping others, we'd come up with ways of factoring both race and class into affirmative action programs. His point is that it is illogical to think that helping poor people equates with helping black people. He sees the whole attempt to focus on class alone as a way of skirting the real issue—an inability to "confront the depth of our racial difficulties" (32). He notes that blacks who are poor have difficulty competing in society not only because of their poverty but also because of their color. He does not think that "remediating class disparities will dissolve our racial difficulties . . . " (33).

APA: Banks (1996) feels that both race and class have to be factored in, even though race matters more. In "Race Matters More," he maintains that proposals to base affirmative action on economic class alone rather than on race ignore fundamental truths about the interplay of race and class. Banks feels that if we really cared about helping others, we'd come up with ways of factoring both race and class into affirmative action programs. His point is that it is illogical to think that helping poor people equates with helping black people. He sees the whole attempt to focus on class alone as a way of skirting the real issue—an inability to "confront the depth of our racial difficulties" (32). He notes that blacks who are poor have difficulty competing in society not only because of their poverty but also because of their color. He does not think that "remediating class disparities will dissolve our racial difficulties . . . " (p. 33).

Guidelines for Bibliographic Citations

Refer to the following pages for quick reference to citation guidelines. For more detailed guidelines, consult the official style guide of either the Modern Language Association or the American Psychological Association. For links to summaries of these guidelines, consult the Web site for this chapter.

1. Book by One Author

MLA: Chandrasekhar, S. *Hungry People and Empty Lands: An Essay on Population Problems and International Tensions.* London: G. Allen & Unwin, 1954.

APA: Chandrasekhar, S. (1954). *Hungry people and empty lands: An essay on population problems and international tensions.* London: G. Allen & Unwin.

2. Book for Two or Three Authors

MLA: Loescher, Gil, and John A. Scanlan. *Calculated Kindness: Refugees and America's Half-Open Door, 1945 to the Present.* New York: The Free Press, 1986.

APA: Loescher, G., & Scanlan, J. A. (1986). *Calculated kindness: Refugees and America's half-open door, 1945 to the present.* New York: The Free Press.

3. Two or More Books by the Same Author(s)

MLA: Nugent, Walter T. K. *Crossings: The Great Transatlantic Migrations. 1870–1914.* Bloomington: Indiana UP, 1992.
———. *Structures of American Social History.* Bloomington: Indiana UP, 1981.
———. *The Tolerant Populists: Kansas, Populism and Nativism.* Chicago: University of Chicago P, 1963.

APA: Nugent, W. T. K. (1963). *The tolerant populists: Kansas, populism and nativism.* Chicago: University of Chicago Press.
Nugent, W. T. K. (1981). *Structures of American social history.* Bloomington, IN: Indiana University Press.
Nugent, W. T. K. (1992). *Crossings: The great transatlantic migrations, 1870–1914.* Bloomington, IN: Indiana University Press.

4. Book by Group or Corporate Author

MLA: International Labour Office. *Migration in Its Various Forms.* Geneva: ILO, 1926.

APA: International Labour Office. (1926). *Migration in its various forms.* Geneva: ILO.

5. Translation

MLA: Avni, Haim. *Argentina and the Jews: A History of Jewish Immigration.* Trans. G. Brand. Tuscaloosa, AL: U of Alabama P, 1991.

APA: Anvi, H. (1991). *Argentina and the Jews: A history of Jewish immigration.* (G. Brand, Trans). Tuscaloosa, AL: University of Alabama Press.

6. Signed Article in a Reference Book

MLA: Scott, Franklin D. "Immigration." *The Encyclopedia Americana.* 1993 ed.

APA: Scott, F. D. (1993). Immigration. In *The Encyclopedia Americana.* (International ed.) (Vol. 14, pp. 803–808). Danbury, CT: Grolier.

7. Unsigned Article in a Reference Book

MLA: "Refugee," *The New Encyclopaedia Britannica*. 1991 ed.

APA: Refugee. (1991). In *The New Encyclopaedia Britannica* (14th ed.) (Vol. 9, p. 998). Chicago: Encyclopaedia Britannica.

8. Introduction, Preface, Foreword, or Afterword

MLA: Glazer, Nathan. Introduction, *Clamor at the Gates: The New American Immigration*. By Glazer. San Francisco: Institute for Contemporary Studies, 1985. 3–13.
Rossant, M. J. Foreword. *Closed Borders: The Contemporary Assault on Freedom of Movement*. By Alan Dowty. New Haven: Yale UP, 1987, ix–x.

APA: Glazer, N. (1985). Introduction: In *Clamor at the gates: The new American immigration*. (pp. 3–13). San Francisco: Institute for Contemporary Studies.
Rossant, M. J. (1987). Foreword. In A. Dowty, *Closed borders: The contemporary assault on freedom of movement*. (pp. ix–x) New Haven: Yale University Press.

9. Government Publications

MLA: United States. Immigration and Naturalization Service. Office of Policy and Planning. *Strategic Plan: Toward INS 2000: Accepting the Challenge*. Washington: GPO, 1994.

APA: Immigration and Naturalization Service. (1994). *Strategic plan: Toward INS 2000: Accepting the challenge*. Washington, DC: Government Printing Office.

10. Signed Article from a Daily Newspaper

MLA: Jouzaitis, Carol. "GOP, Business Split on Immigration Issue." *Chicago Tribune* 27 Feb. 1996: 4.

APA: Jouzaitis, C. (1994, February 27). GOP, business split on immigration issue. *The Chicago Tribune*, p. 4.

11. Editorial, Letter to the Editor, Review

MLA: "Don't Bar All Immigrants." Editorial, *USA Today* 29 Feb. 1996: A11.
Altshuler, Linda. "Barnum Didn't Say It." Letter. *New York Times* 15 July 1996: A 12.
Wolfe, Alan. "Displaced Persons." Rev. of *Fresh Blood* by Sanford J. Ungar and *American Dreaming: Immigrant Life on the Margins* by Sarah J. Mahler. *New York Times Book Review* 17 Dec. 1995: 29.

APA: Don't bar all immigrants. (1996, February 29). [Editorial]. *USA Today*, p. A11.
Altshuler, L. (1996, July 15). Barnum didn't say it. [Letter to the editor]. the *New York Times*, p. A12.
Wolfe, A. (1995, December 17). Displaced Persons. [Review of the books *Fresh blood & American dreaming: Immigrant life on the margins*]. the *New York Times Book Review*, p. 29.

12. Unsigned Article from a Daily Newspaper

MLA: "Tech Firms Oppose a Ban on Immigrants." *USA Today* 28 Feb. 1996: B4.

APA: Tech Firms Oppose a Ban on Immigrants. (1996, February 28). *USA Today*, p. B4.

13. Signed Article from a Weekly Magazine

MLA: Smith, Norman. "Bosnian Asylum-Seekers Targeted by Home Office." *New Statesman & Society*, 24 Nov. 1995: 9.

APA: Smith, N. (1995, November 24). Bosnian asylum-seekers targeted by home office. *New Statesman & Society*, 9.

14. Signed Article from a Monthly of Bimonthly Periodical

MLA: Lequerica, Martha. "Stress in Immigrant Families with Handicapped Children: A Child Advocacy Approach." *American Journal of Orthopsychiatry* Oct. 1993: 545–52. Weiner, Myron. "Nations Without Borders: The Gifts of Folk Gone Abroad." *Foreign Affairs* Mar.–Apr. 1996: 128–34.

APA: Lequerica, M. (1993, October). Stress in immigrant families with handicapped children: A child advocacy approach. *American Journal of Orthopsychiatry*, 545–52. Weiner, M. (1996, March/April). Nations without borders: The gifts of folk gone abroad. *Foreign Affairs*, 128–34.

15. Unsigned Article from a Weekly or Monthly Periodical

MLA: "No Room at Europe's Inn." *The Economist* 9 Dec. 1995: 53–54.

APA: No Room at Europe's Inn. (1995, December 9). *The Economist*, pp. 53–54.

16. Article in a Journal with Continuous Pagination

> **MLA:** Massey, Douglas S. "The New Immigration and Ethnicity in the United States." *Population and Development Review* 21 (1995): 631–52.

> **APA:** Massey, D. S. (1995). The new immigration and ethnicity in the United States. *Population and Development Review, 21,* 631–652.

17. Article in a Journal That Pages Each Issue Separately

> **MLA:** McKelvey, Robert S., and John A. Webb. "Unaccompanied Status as a Risk Factor in Vietnamese Amerasians." *Social Science & Medicine* 41.2 (1995): 261–66.

> **APA:** McKelvey, R. S., & Webb, J. A. (1995). Unaccompanied status as a risk factor in Vietnamese Amerasians. *Social Science & Medicine, 41*(2), 261–266.

GUIDELINES FOR ELECTRONIC CITATION

The best way to begin learning how to cite electronic sources is to realize that they follow the same general principles for in-text citation and works cited that are used for print sources in your field. That is, MLA electronic citation guidelines follow the guidelines for MLA books and journals, and APA guidelines are the starting point for citation of electronic sources in APA style.

Guidelines for citation are still in flux, but standards are beginning to emerge. New recommendations regarding online citations are explained in the *MLA Style Manual* (1998). The MLA has posted its guidelines for electronic citations at <http://www.mla.org/main_stl.htm#sources>. You can find APA's guidelines at <http://www.apa.org/journals/webref.html>. But since this site presents only minimal suggestions for electronic citation, many researchers continue to follow suggested Web guidelines popularized by Xia Li and Nancy Crane <http://www.uvm.edu/~xli/reference/estyles.html>.

If you publish your research paper on the Web, you will be able to include hyperlinks to Web sources throughout the paper. At the end of the paper, in the references section, you should create links from your Web sources to the respective Web sites. In addition, you should create links from your in-text citations to the full source in the Works Cited or Reference sections.

For example: Clicking Greenman at the end of the following paragraph (from the sample search paper included in this text), should link the reader to the Greenman reference in the Works Cited section.

> Some groups argue that affirmative action isn't really needed in some parts of the country. One group of students . . . has argued that diversity would exist on their campus without what they see as offensive "racially based guidelines," since they live in a place with a mix of cultures (<u>Greenman</u>).

Works Cited

Greenman, Ted. "Students Against Affirmative Action and for Equality." 29 Aug. 1996. 17 Sep. 1996 <<u>http:www.cwo.com/~tag/saaae.html</u>>.

In the Works Cited section, clicking on Greenman should take the reader directly to the "Students Against Affirmative Action and for Equality" Web page.

A caution: don't limit yourself to Web resources just because it is handy for the reader to be able to read the entire source by clicking on a link. If you want to provide the reader with information on the books and journal articles not available on the Web, you could summarize that and link to the summaries. Your research paper should include the most appropriate Web sources possible, whether those sources are in the library or on the Web.

General Guidelines

For electronic sources, you need the following information:

- Author's name.
- Title of Web source (or scholarly project, online book, etc.) or LISTSERV posting (or subject of e-mail message).
- Title of Web site [if the page is part of a larger resource with its own title].
- Date of publication or posting of Web source.
- Publication information (such as volume and page numbers of print versions of the source—if listed, name of listserv, name of professional organization sponsoring site, etc.).
- Date you accessed the Web source.
- Web address (URL).

Use the charts provided on pp. 124, 126, and 127 to record this information for each of your sources.

If the source you are citing exists in print format as well as in electronic format, you must provide readers with the source information (e.g., volume, issue, and page number) for the print material before providing the Web information. You are not expected to consult the print source.

In all cases (whether APA or MLA) you need to indicate the date the source was first published or last revised as well as the date that you accessed this source. The version of the Web source that you saw may bear little resemblance to the way the site looks at the time someone reads your paper. By providing the date you accessed the source, you indicate to your reader that you have tried to be as accurate as possible, but are not responsible for changes after the date in your reference. Because Web sites are not permanent, you should make copies of sources you use in you paper. The guidelines for MLA and APA electronic citation are explained in the following section.

MLA Electronic Citation Style

The MLA Handbook for Writers of Research Papers, fourth edition, gives considerable coverage to electronic citation style. The style that MLA recommends includes angle brackets <> to enclose web addresses (URLs).

General Format

Author, title, date of publication, and date of access.

> Rodrigues, Dawn. The Research Paper and the World Wide Web Site. 9 Oct. 1996. 25 Feb 1998 <http://www.prenhall.com/rodrigues>.

MLA guidelines require that you include the following information:

- Author, editor, compiler or translator (whichever is appropriate).
- Date of publication or posting.
- Number of pages or paragraphs, if they are so numbered.
- Name of institution or organization sponsoring the Web site.
- Name of list or forum followed by the words Online posting.
- Name of sponsoring site if citing a subsection of a larger site.
- Date of access.
- URL with angle brackets.

Examples

Web Pages That Are Part of Larger Projects

> Gilman, Charlotte Perkins. "The Yellow Wall-Paper." *The American Reader Survey Site*. Ed. Daniel Anderson. 3 Sep. 1996. U of Texas. 23 Mar. 1998 <http://www.utexas.edu/~danderson.html>.

Personal Site

Rodrigues, Dawn. Home page. 3 Mar. 1998
<http://www.utb.edu/~drodrigu>.

Site with a Sponsoring Organization

Guidelines for Committees. 2 Feb. 1998. National Council of Teachers of
English. 23 Mar. 1998. <http://www.ncte.org>.

Article in a Reference Database

Recchio, Thomas E. "Some Versions of Critical Pedagogy," *College English*
7. 58 (1996): 845+. PROQUEST. 2 Feb. 1998. ISSN: 00100994.

or

Recchio, Thomas E. "Some Versions of Critical Pedagogy," College English (7) 58 (1996): 845+. PROQUEST. 2 Feb. 1998
<http://www.proquest.umi.com>.

or

"Fresco." Britannica Online. Vers. 97.1.1. Mar. 1997. Encyclopaedia Britannica. 29 Mar. 1997 <http://www.eb.com:180>.

Scholarly Project

Women of the Romantic Period. Ed. WORP Developers, Computer Writing and Research Labs. Apr. 2 February 1997. UT Austin. 23 May 1999
<http://www.cwrl.utexas.edu/~worp/>.

Professional Site

Modern Language Association. 1 May 1999. <http://www.mla.org/>.

Book

Lofting, Hugh. *The Voyages of Dr. Doolittle.* Online Books Page. Jan. 1998
Carnegie Mellon University. 1 April 1999
<http://www.cs.cmu.edu/People/spok/prize.html#newbery>.

Poem

Nesbit, E[dith]. "Marching Song." Ballads and Lyrics of Socialism. London,
1908. Victorian Women Writers Project. Ed Perry Willett. Apr. 1997.
Indiana U. 26 Apr. 1997 <http://www.indiana/edu/~letrs/vwwp/
nesbit/ballsoc.html#p9>.

Article or Review in a Journal

Voekely, Swen. "Review of Broken English: Dialects and the Politics of
Language in Renaissance Writings." Early Modern Literary Studies
4.1 (May 1998): 5 pars. 2 April 1999 <http://purl.oclc.org/emls/
04-1/rev_voe2.html>.

WWW, Telnet, and FTP Addresses

AUTHOR	TITLE	TITLE OF COMPLETE PUBLICATION, IF APPLICABLE	DATE OF PUBLICATION OR LAST REVISION	HTTP: ADDRESS (INCLUDE ADDITIONAL DIRECTIONS, IF NEEDED)	DATES OF ACCESS

Article in a Magazine

> Mack, Tracy L. "What Can You Learn from a Rainbow?" *Interracial Voice* March–April 1999. 2 May 1999 <http://www.webcom.com/~intvoice/tracy.html>.

Work from a Subscription Service

> Seago, Kate. "Internet Keeps Handbook of Term Paper Style in State of Flux." *The Dallas Morning News*. (3 March 1998): 22 Electric Lib. 23 April 1999 <http://www.elibrary.com/>.

> "Making Print and Online Media Work for You." Media Professional Newsletter 4.10 5 April 1999. America Online. 4 May 1999. Keywords: Writing and Publishing; Media Professional Newsletter.

Posting to a Discussion List (*listserv, newsgroup, or forum*)

> Carbone, Nick. "RE: Question." Online posting. 21 Apr. 1999. Alliance for Computers and Writing Listserv. 6 May 1997 <http://www.arts.ubc.ca/english/iemls/shak/>.

E-mail

> Seiple, Carl. "Kutztown." E-mail to the author. 20 Feb. 1998.

Synchronous Communication

> Crump, Eric, and Dawn Rodrigues. MOO conversation. 20 Feb. 1998 <http://mud.ncte.org:8888/>.

APA Electronic Citation Style

The American Psychological Association has begun to develop guidelines for electronic citation; however, at the time of this printing, their guidelines have not yet been published in the APA Style Manual and are not followed as widely as the guidelines recommended later in this chapter.

APA tends to be much more concerned about providing readers with a way of retrieving the exact document. They urge you to provide as much information as possible to allow a reader to access the source. Thus, if you have used a proprietary database such as Encyclopaedia Britannica, include not only the reference number, but the URL, too. If you have used a system other than the Web, indicate the exact way that you accessed your source, even if there is no standard citation format provided for your needs. If you have accessed a source through a gopher or FTP information databases, model your citation on the examples given below for the World Wide Web, being careful to indicate the exact path. A similar format can be used to cite gopher or FTP sources, as long as the medium and the path are sufficiently identified.

Mailing List, Newsgroup, and E-mail Addresses

AUTHOR'S NAME OR LOGIN ID IF NAME IS NOT AVAILABLE	AUTHOR'S E-MAIL ADDRESS	SUBJECT OF MESSAGE	DATE MESSAGE SENT	ADDRESS OF LIST OR USENET GROUP	DATE MESSAGE WAS ACCESSED

Collecting CD-ROM and Online Databases

AUTHOR	TITLE OF WORK	TITLE OF COMPLETE PUBLICA- TION, IF APPLICABLE	DATE OF PUBLICA- TION OR LAST REVISION	TITLE OF ELECTRONIC WORK	MEDIUM	INFOR- MATION SUPPLIER (E.G., ERIC)	FILE ID OR HTTP ADDRESS	DATE OF ACCESS (IF REGULARLY REVISED)

Here are the main features of the APA Guidelines as posted at the APA Web site <http://www.apa.org/journals/webref.html>:

■ Begin by providing all information that would be standard in a printed APA reference, then follow with the Web page title and address (URL).

Example
Rosenthal, R. (1995). State of New Jersey v. Margaret Kelly Michaels: An overview [Abstract]. *Psychology, Public Policy, and Law, 1*, 247–271. Retrieved January 25, 1996 from the World Wide Web: http://www.apa.org/journals/ab1.html

■ In most cases, include a statement such as the following: "Retrieved [date] from the World Wide Web: http://

Example
Retrieved March 5, 1998 from the World Wide Web: http://www.ncte.org

■ After the title of the Web site, enclose a word or a phrase in brackets to indicate the nature of the publication: [Newspaper], [Selected stories on line], [Abstract].

Example
National Council of Teachers of English (1998, March 3). CCCCs program available on the Web [Announcement posted on the World Wide Web]. Urbana, Illinois: Author. Retrieved March 5, 1998 from the World Wide Web: http://www.ncte.org

■ Do not put a period at the end of the sentence. (The reader might think that the period is part of the URL.)
■ Do not list personal e-mail messages or messages from a synchronous conversation in a MOO or on a forum in the References section. They are treated as private correspondence, and referenced only as in-text citations, just as standard APA style treats personal correspondence.

Example
R. Rodrigues (personal communication, March 28, 1998).

Alternate APA Electronic Style

You may wish to follow the Web guidelines developed by librarians Xia Li and Nancy Crane. Their extensive guidelines have been published in "Electronic Style: An Expanded Guide to Citing Electronic Information" (*Information Today*, 1996). Because Li and Crane's guidelines are used widely in a variety of disciplines, I have chosen to include them in the samples provided in this section and in the References section of the APA research paper (p. 187).

APA style guidelines require that you provide a reader with exact access information. If you cannot provide readers with a way of retrieving the material you have cited, then you should provide the primary source in an appendix. If you want to quote from an informal MOO conversation, you can; but you do not include the source in your References list. If you think you might want to quote from a given MOO conversation, be sure to "log" or capture the conversation so that you will have a record of it if anyone asks to see the entire transcript. Check the software on your computer to see how it logs the results of an entire online session.

Although Li and Crane recommend using the term *online* in an Internet citation, the guidelines that follow recommend merely indicating the Web address. Some readers will access these resources in different ways (Telnetting directly, using an FTP program, etc.); providing the URL seems sufficient, since it gives everyone the information needed to locate the resource. An example of Li and Crane's format and that recommended here will illustrate the differences.

Li and Crane recommend the following format:

Johnson, T. (1994, December 5). Indigenous people are now more combative, organized. *Miami Herald* [Online], p. 29SA (22 paragraphs). Available: gopher://americas.fiu.edu70/00/herald/herald.417 [1995, July 16].

We recommend the format below, which omits *online*:

Johnson, T. (1994, December 5). Indigenous people are now more combative, organized. *Miami Herald*, p. 29SA (22 paragraphs). Available: gopher://summit.fiu.edu/gopher://americas.fiu.edu70/00/herald/herald.417 [1995, July 16].

The following is the general format to follow:

Author/editor. (Year). Title (edition), [Type of medium, if not a Web source.} Producer or publisher (for proprietary material). Availability information. [Access date].

If you are citing a Gopher, Web, Telnet, or FTP site, provide the URL immediately after the word *available* (e.g., Available: http://www.prenhall/com/rodrigues). For CD-ROM databases [proprietary sources] or other electronic media, provide the producer or publisher and identifying information that would enable a reader to locate the material you accessed. Remember to provide an access date at the end of the citation.

General Format for Web Addresses

Author/editor. (Year). *Title* (edition) and publication information. Available: http:// or gopher: // or telnet: // [Access date].

If no publication date is available, write "No date." Use the same general format for all Web addresses (http, Telnet, Gopher, and FTP). End with the access date. Do not put a period after the address. If you are citing an online journal or newspaper, you should indicate the pages from which you have taken your quotation; in the References list, provide the number of paragraphs.

Web Addresses

Li, X., & Crane, N. (1996). Bibliographic format for citing electronic information. Available: http://www.uvm.edu/~xli/reference/estyles.html [1996, April 29].

Greenman, T. (1996, August 29). Students against affirmative action and for equality. Available: http://www.cwo.com/~tag/saaae.html [1996, September 17].

Johnson, T. (1994, December 5). Indigenous people are now more combative, organized. *Miami Herald*. p. 29SA (22 paragraphs). Available: gopher://summit.fiu.edu/MiamiHerald—Summit-Related Articles/12/05/95—Indigenous People Now More Combative, Organized [1995, July 16].

Noguera, P. (1996). A popular movement for social justice. *In Motion Magazine* (20 paragraphs). Available: http://www.inmotionmagazine.com/pedro2.html [1996, September 24].

Rockwell, P. (1996, April 17). Angry white guys for affirmative action. Available: http://www.inmotionmagazine.com/rocka.html [1996, April 30].

Sanchez, C. (1996, January 13). Future of affirmative action in higher education. National Public Radio. *Electric Library*, p. B5 (9 paragraphs). Available: http://www.elibrary.com [1996, October 1].

Viviano, F. (1995, May/June). The new Mafia order. *Mother Jones Magazine* (72 paragraphs). Available: http://www.mojones.com/MOTHER_JONES/MJ95/viviano.html [1995, July 17].

General Format for Mailing List, Newsgroup, and E-mail Citations

Use a similar font for mailing list, newsgroup, e-mail citations, and synchronous conversations, making slight adaptations as needed.

Mailing List or Newsgroup

Author. (Year, month, day). Subject of message. *Discussion List* or *Newsgroup* [Type of medium]. Available: [address or directions for retrieving from archive] [Access date].
Slade, R. (1996, March 26) UNIX made easy. Available: news://alt.books.reviews [1996, March 31].

E-mail

Author (Sender's e-mail address). (Year, month day). *Subject of Message.* E-mail to receiver's name. (Receiver's e-mail address).
Rodrigues, D. (drodrigues@utbl.utb.edu). (1996, October 5) Ocean Creek Institute. E-mail to Susan Lang (slang@siu.edu).

Ask the sender for permission to quote a message sent to you. APA guidelines recommend that you give the e-mail addresses of the sender and the receiver. Let the sender know that you have included his or her e-mail address in your References list.

Synchronous (Real-Time) Conversations

Speaker. Type of Communication. [Access date].
Harnack, A. Group Discussion. Available:
telnet://moo.du.org/port=8888 [1996, April 4].

General Format for CD-ROM and Database Citations

Many libraries have put their CD-ROM database collection online. In other cases, libraries subscribe to online databases for their campus. Someone who is not a registered student cannot use the privately owned databases. If the database is available on the Internet, even though it is available only to registered users, give the URL. If the database is available in another medium (e.g., CD-ROM), then indicate that medium.

Author. (Year, month day). Title. [edition and volume number] [Type of medium], page cited and page numbers. Available: Supplier/Database name (Database identifier or access number) [Access date].
Oxford English dictionary computer file: On compact disc (2nd ed.), [CD-ROM]. (1992). Available: Oxford UP [1995, May 27].
Goodwin, M.E. (1992). An obituary to affirmative action and a call for self-reliance. (ERIC Document Reproduction Service [CD-ROM], no. ED357998).
Goodwin, M.E. (1992). An obituary to affirmative action and a call for self-reliance. (ERIC Document Reproduction Service, No. ED357998) Available telnet://ERIC@sklib.usask.ca:23/ (Log in as ERIC). [1996, October 22].

The ERIC Document Reproduction Service collections are available in many different formats, including CD-ROMs and Web sites. The two previous examples illustrate how you would cite either of the two ERIC sources. Note that if you are citing an Internet source, the only indication of the type of medium you are using is the presence of a URL.

Howell, V., & Carlton, B. (1993, August 29). Growing up tough: New generation fights for its life: Inner-city youths live by rule of vengeance. *Birmingham News* [CD-ROM], p. 1A (10 pp.) Available: 1994 SIRS/SIRS 1993 Youth/Volume 4/Article 56A [1995, July 16].

Suggestions for Citing Web Sources:

- ■ Examine URLs carefully so that you are sure you are copying them correctly. If possible, copy the URL from the online source and paste it into your note-cards so that you don't misspell it.

- ■ Note both the date the item was created and the access date (the date you retrieved the source).

- ■ If the Web source you are quoting is a journal, current guidelines suggest that you include the number of paragraphs if they are numbered for you (just as, for a printed source, you indicated the number of pages).

- ■ Ask the author of an e-mail message for permission before you cite it. Note: Although Li and Crane recommend including e-mail references, the trend in APA style is to treat e-mail as personal correspondence, which in standard APA style is *not* included in the References list, though it is noted in the in-text citation.

FORMATTING THE RESEARCH PAPER: MLA AND APA EXAMPLES

Different documentation styles also have different styles of page formatting. Most research papers do not require title pages, but if your instructor asks for one, follow our suggested format. A sample title page, abstract page, first page, and reference page in APA style appear after the MLA research paper.

MLA Style First Page without a Title Page

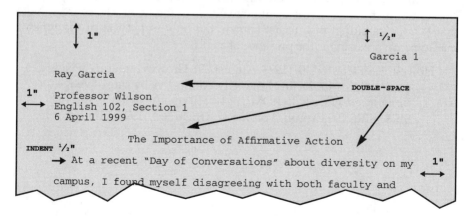

MLA Style Title Page

CENTER TITLE
1/3 DOWN THE PAGE

Affirmative Action: Help or Hindrance?

by   DOUBLE-SPACE

Ray Garcia   "BY" AND NAME

DOUBLE-SPACE

English 102, Section 1   COURSE, SECTION

Professor Wilson   NAME OF PROFESSOR

April 6, 1999   DATE

1"

MLA Style First Page with a Separate Title Page

Garcia 1 ↕ ½"

↕ 1"

Affirmative Action: Help or Hindrance?

INDENT ½" → At a recent "Day of Conversations" about diversity

on my campus, I found myself disagreeing with both fac-

ulty and other students on whether affirmative action in

university admission policies was beneficial or harmful.

This experience led me to realize that I needed to

explore affirmative action in greater depth. I wanted to

learn whether the lukewarm attitude toward affirmative

action and diversity issues at my campus was justified

and whether the nation's policies toward affirmative

←→ 1"   action had changed. What is the current status of affir-   1" ←→

mative action programs nationally? Have the courts

changed their attitudes toward affirmative action? And if

affirmative action programs in their current form are

being threatened by legislation and court decisions, are

there any viable alternatives for reducing discrimina-

tion in admission policies and promoting diversity among

the student body?

Some background about the history of affirmative

action may be helpful. Affirmative action is a series of

programs put into place during Lyndon Johnson's presi-

↕ 1"

Garcia 2

dency, programs that were designed to correct inequities

in college enrollments based upon previous disadvantages

that minorities as groups had experienced. The arguments

in favor of affirmative action stress the need to remedy

the effects of past discrimination against minorities

and women. These remedies include:

• special admissions programs,

• special scholarship programs, and

• changes in the curriculum.

Changes in the curriculum were not mandated by law but

were the result of a belief on the part of faculty and

students that the curriculum should not discriminate

against minorities and women by excluding their history,

literature, and cultures from the curriculum in favor of

the traditional white European content of the curricu-

lum. Because curricular changes were not required by

laws or policies, I will concentrate upon admission and

scholarship programs in this paper.

President Lyndon Johnson issued Executive Order

11246 calling for "affirmative action" in the actions of

federal contractors, colleges, universities, and the

federal government. It was intended to increase the num-

Garcia 3

bers of women and minorities participating in the work

of federal contractors and the federal government and in

obtaining a university education (Lappe 97). Johnson

explained the need for affirmative action in a June 1965

address at Howard University, noting that freedom of

opportunity doesn't immediately level the playing field.

> You do not take a man who for years has been hob-
>
> bled by chains, liberate him, and bring him to the
>
> starting line of a race, saying "you are free to
>
> compete with all others," and still justly believe
>
> you have been completely fair. Thus it is not
>
> enough to open the gates of opportunity. (qtd. in
>
> Lappe 97)

For over three decades, affirmative action programs

have been in place, and, even though they haven't dra-

matically increased the number of minority students and

faculty, they have helped increase the numbers. If noth-

ing else, the debates about affirmative action programs

have led to more conversations on campus about diversity

in all of its forms. More importantly, the existence of

these programs, by bringing more students from different

Garcia 4

ethnic groups together with white students in normal

activities, has developed students' respect for diver-

sity and more faculty efforts to diversify the curricu-

lum. One study, for example, found that students from

all racial and ethnic groups showed strong support for

diversity efforts in the curriculum (Lopez 33).

Since that time, a number of court cases have

tested affirmative action, with a few key cases. For

example, in 1978, the U. S. Supreme Court held that the

Medical School at the University of California at Davis

had discriminated against the race (white) of an appli-

cant by favoring other students on the basis of race.

Commonly referred to as "the Bakke case," the Court held

that racial preferences were only appropriate when an

institution could demonstrate a history of past discrim-

ination and only for the purposes of correcting the dis-

crimination. (University of California Regents v. Bakke)

Ever since the inception of affirmative action,

there has been much disagreement about whether it cor-

rects for discrimination or whether it simply causes

discrimination against another group. Lately, affirmative

action policies have been increasingly attacked in the

courts. Arthur Levin, President of Columbia Teachers

College, said recently, "What we'll see in the next few

years . . . is that unless there's enormous pressure

behind affirmative action it's going to fall off the

tray" (qtd. in Sanchez 32).

A series of court challenges has threatened affirma-

tive action programs or seriously undermined them in

many colleges and universities. In March 1996, the U.S.

Court of Appeals for the Fifth Circuit, hearing the

appeal on Hopwood v. Texas, ruled that the University of

Texas could not base preferential racial or ethnic

admissions upon a claim that the University was trying

to remedy past social discrimination. (Hopwood v. The

State of Texas) That is, University officials could not

prove that the University itself had discriminated

against certain groups of students. Before this Hopwood

decision, all colleges and universities in the Fifth

Circuit area (Texas, Louisiana, and Mississippi) were

able to recruit minority students using special affirma-

tive action criteria. Schools could set up affirmative

action programs even if they themselves had never prac-

ticed or been accused of discrimination. As long as the

Garcia 6

minorities had suffered from discriminatory policies or

practices in the state or region of the country, indi-

vidual institutions were able to help redress past

wrongs through their affirmative action programs (Jachik

and Lederman).

On July 1, 1996, the U.S. Supreme Court decided not

to review the Hopwood decision of the 5th Circuit Court.

For opponents of affirmative action, this signaled that

the Court would not support preferential treatment on

the basis of race or ethnicity. For supporters of affir-

mative action, the Hopwood decision and the Supreme

Court's decision not to review it did not overturn the

Bakke decision but simply supported a lower court ruling

that had determined that a particular affirmative action

program was inappropriate. (Online NewsHour)

A second important court decision relates to Cali-

fornia's Proposition 209, which blocked affirmative

action throughout California. In 1997, the 9th U.S. Cir-

cuit Court of Appeals ruled that the Proposition was

constitutional, and, again, the U.S. Supreme Court

decided not to hear an appeal. Again supporters of affir-

mative action argue that the Proposition goes far beyond

what the Court may have intended and believe the Court's action leaves the issues surrounding affirmative action policies still open, still active, and still subject to future court action (Biskupik).

Court rulings are not the only indication that affirmative action programs are in trouble. In recent years, there's been an erosion of interest in affirmative action, even by minorities themselves. Critics of affirmative action have crafted many arguments against it. They point out the following problems with affirmative action programs:

• Preferential treatment for minorities creates a different kind of prejudice and a new kind of discrimination--a discrimination against white males (Rockwell). The weakened economy in California, with fewer jobs in higher education now available, has stimulated greater support for anti-affirmative action initiatives. White males think they'll have more chance for employment if minorities do not get preferential treatment.

• Affirmative action stigmatizes minorities who benefit from it. (Even those who may be qualified enough to be hired or admitted without affirmative action are

Garcia 8

assumed to have been hired because of their minority

status and so feel the stigma.)

• Affirmative action ignores individual merit.

• Affirmative action gives minorities excuses for not

trying harder (Goodwin).

• Affirmative action doesn't really work well anyway.

(According to a study at the Tomàs Rivera Center, the

percentage of Latino faculty with the University of

California system has increased only minimally since

affirmative action programs began in the sixties.)

(Achieving)

• Affirmative action benefits the most qualified and privi-

leged people from the disadvantaged groups, leaving

the others as they always were; it's the upper-middle-

class minorities who tend to get into college or get

jobs that affirmative action programs make available.

• Affirmative action programs aren't really needed in

every part of the country. One group of students at

the University of California (Students against Affirma-

tive Action and for Equality) has argued that diver-

sity would exist on their campus without what they see

as offensive "racially-based guidelines," since they

live in a place with a mix of cultures (Greenman).

For all these reasons, affirmative action has been losing supporters. As R. Richard Banks argues, there is an increasing reluctance of intellectuals and politicians to identify social problems as explicitly racial programs (Banks). The only arguments that have gained momentum are those that suggest that perhaps class rather than race should be used as the main criteria for preference in college and on the job.

Two key alternatives to affirmative action have been proposed. The first suggests that inequity be addressed by looking at socioeconomic class rather than race. The second, responding to the anti-affirmative action sentiment in the country, is an even bolder maneuver—favoring no one, but having as a goal a multitalented student body that would end up being more diverse as a result of recruiting for different skills. I discuss the two below.

Richard Kahlenberg offers a choice of several ways to address class rather than race in college admissions, ranging from a simple reporting of family income to a more complex series of calculations based on factors such as the neighborhood where a student lives, the

quality of the high school that the student may have

attended, and family income. His argument is based on

the research that shows that lower socioeconomic class

blacks have not seen any real benefit from affirmative

action.

Not everyone agrees that it would be better to base

affirmative action on class rather than race. Some note

that poor whites outnumber the poor of other races. Fur-

ther, whites and Asians have historically scored higher

on SAT exams, so socioeconomically poor whites and

Asians might benefit disproportionately more than poor

blacks, Hispanics, and American Indians if class deter-

mined admissions instead of race (Dickerson).

Banks feels that both race and class have to be

factored in, even though race matters more. In "Race

Matters More," he maintains that proposals to base affir-

mative action on economic class alone rather than on

race ignore fundamental truths about the interplay of

race and class. Banks feels that, if we really cared

about helping others, we would come up with ways of fac-

toring both race and class into affirmative action pro-

grams. He sees the whole attempt to focus on class alone
as a way of skirting the real issue--an inability to
"confront the depth of our racial difficulties." He notes
that blacks who are poor have difficulty competing in
society not only because of their poverty, but also
because of their color. He does not think that "remediating class disparities will dissolve our racial difficulties."

The second alternative to affirmative action programs as they have traditionally been practiced was
started by the University of Texas-Austin, a highly
selective school, after the Hopwood decision. Instead of
giving a certain number of slots to certain classes of
students who may not meet SAT standards, the University
announced that it would begin reviewing all applications
individually. Subjective criteria including such characteristics as family background and responses to written
essay prompts would be reviewed by a committee (University of Texas C7). With this system, race would count as
one factor in putting together a freshman class that is
diversified. This approach would moderate the inevitable
results if high test scores alone are used for admis-

Garcia 12

sions decisions, and resembles the practices of Ivy

League and other elite private schools of taking into

account many factors, including geographical distribu-

tion of the freshman class.

As it turned out, the 1997 Legislature of Texas

found its own way around the Hopwood decision. They

passed a law (SB 1419) that allows any student in the

top 10 percent of his or her class, in any high school,

regardless of SAT or ACT scores, regardless of grade

point average, and regardless of other standardized mea-

sures, to be eligible for admission to any public higher

education institution in Texas. In this way, a Hispanic

or an African American student from an educationally

weak school district would be admitted based upon com-

petitive merit within his or her school district. This

would enable the state universities to admit students

who appear to have the ability to succeed, regardless of

how well or poorly they might compare on standardized

measures with other students from across the State--and

would do so regardless of race or ethnicity.

Clearly, preserving affirmative action without dis-

criminating against any racial or ethnic group can take

many forms that may all be open to some legal challenge.

But just as important as these programs is the need to

continue work on the prejudicial and discriminatory

mindset that many individuals have grown up with. If

affirmative action based on race is replaced by any of

the suggested alternatives--class, rank within a school,

or multiple criteria--there still is no guarantee that

multiethnic and multiracial respect will be present on

the campuses.

The real issue is deeper than the arguments over

affirmative action seem to imply. The problems of race

and ethnicity remain. And while affirmative action pro-

grams and their alternatives may provide access to

higher education for many formerly denied that access,

affirmative action has other purposes. In particular,

these programs have been intended to foster so-called

"diversity" on campus, including diversity in the cur-

riculum.[1] These programs need to be kept alive.

[1]"Diversity" is a term used to refer to the value of having people from diverse backgrounds and cultures together on campus.
Diversity efforts on campus are geared to reducing prejudice and
to promoting an understanding of different cultures. Often,
diversity programs support multicultural programming on campus
and promote curricular changes that reflect the ethnic background
of students on a given campus.

Garcia 14

Unfortunately, universities seem particularly apa-
thetic. Perhaps a key reason that there's been little
alarm and worry is that schools have too many other
problems right now. An NPR interview with various administrators indicated that universities and colleges may
very easily not contest the challenges since they are
having to contend with increasingly difficult budget and
accountability challenges from their constituents. As
Claudio Sanchez put it, "The end of affirmative action in
the University of California system . . . has exposed some
deep-seated misgivings about racial preferences in hiring and admissions."

Noting the need to improve the educational conditions for poor children, Jack Kemp suggests a new role
for affirmative action, that of "ending the educational
monopoly that makes poor public school students into
pawns of the educational bureaucracy." Similarly, Clint
Bolick, the litigation director of the Institute of Justice, has argued against racial preferences as a form of
affirmative action, but has argued that universities
could truly support affirmative action if they worked to
improve public education, especially public education in

inner city high schools and illiteracy rates among black

high school students. "What I hope the practical effect

[of the Supreme Court not hearing the Hopwood decision]

will be is that colleges, instead of using racial pref-

erences, are going to start to solve the underlying

problems. . . . That is what affirmative action ought to

address." [Online NewsHour}

What will happen if nothing is done to preserve at

least the diversity initiatives related to affirmative

action? As Pedro Noguera points out, "Without a policy

that holds universities and employers accountable for

who they admit, the pledge to not discriminate is mean-

ingless" (50). People who have grown up with prejudicial

attitudes toward other groups do not change their belief

systems easily. Without some programs to bring minori-

ties and economically poor students into college, soci-

ety will lose.

Columnist and Senator Bill Bradley is convinced

that racism and discrimination won't go away easily

because "many people hold values that allow them to

defend the social advantage they have based on being

upper-class whites" (10). Unfortunately, Bradley's

Garcia 16

observations may be too accurate.

Interestingly, the Hopwood decision and Proposition 209, coupled with the Supreme Court's refusal to hear appeals of the lower court decisions, have not started a rush to end affirmative action everywhere. In Houston, for example, at the end of November 1997, voters approved keeping the City's affirmative action plan. And equally interestingly, it was because business leaders in Houston led the opposition to ending affirmative action. It appeared that, if the universities of Texas could not stand firm on affirmative action, business would. In a heavily Hispanic city, business leaders apparently felt that opposing affirmative action would hurt business (Barnes).

Earlier mandates for affirmative action have helped decrease discrimination and prejudice by bringing those issues to the forefront of campus life, but it took more than 20 years to begin to see the benefits of affirmative action programs. Looking at the gains of minority enrollment in colleges is telling: "National enrollment figures illustrate that enrollment of people of color has grown from negligible figures when schools were segregated to about 20% of the nation's post-secondary educa-

tion students" (Lappe 47). That pattern won't continue

if affirmative action programs end.

What can be done? As Goodwin notes, apparently

agreeing with Clint Bolick's point that affirmative

action should address the root causes of problems that

affirmative action was designed to address, what was

needed when Lyndon Johnson issued his Executive Order--

and still needed today--is equalization of resources and

facilities, not just affirmative action policies. He

calls for a new political vision that "asks people to

engage each other" (2).

My research into the issues of affirmative action,

especially as they apply to colleges and universities,

indicates that this complex issue cannot simply be about

admissions preferences. Colleges and universities have a

responsibility to lead the nation in addressing the edu-

cational imbalances that exist as a result of previous

discrimination, even if discrimination may not exist in

the same ways that it once did. They should not only

encourage more substantive discussions of the issues,

but they should also work toward overtly addressing the

Garcia 18

unequal opportunities that exist in this nation: prepar-

ing better teachers, working with school districts to

strengthen education for all students, instilling a

sense of public service in all their graduates.

The bottom line is this: college administrators,

faculty, and students know that racial and ethnic issues

and tensions have not been solved by affirmative action

programs alone. Admissions preferences may have benefited

students who were victims of unequal educational oppor-

tunities, but they have done so at the expense of the

goodwill of many white students and citizens who view

them as one more form of discrimination.

Special programs such as our "Days of Conversa-

tions" must keep these issues alive. But long after

these days have ended, administrators, faculty, and stu-

dents must commit themselves to real affirmative action,

actions designed to make the United States and the world

a better place for all people, regardless of their

racial or ethnic histories.

Works Cited

"Achieving Faculty Diversity: Debunking the Myths."
   Diversity Digest 24 Dec. 1998
   <http:www.inform.umd.edu/diversityweb/Digest/F97/
   research.html>.

Alicea, I.P. "Dismantling Affirmative Action." *Journal of
   Blacks in Higher Education* 5.19 (1995): 4.

Banks, R. Richard. "Race Matters Most." *Los Angeles
   Times* 22 May 1995: B5. Electric Library. 17 April
   1996 <http://www.elibrary.com>.

Barnes, Julian E. "Houston Slows the Tidal Wave." *U.S.
   News* 17 November 1997 <http://www.usnews.com/
   usnews/issue/971117/17affi.htm>.

Biskupic, Joan. "Affirmative Action Ban Is Left Intact by
   Supreme Court." *Washington Post* 4 November 1997:
   A01. <http://www.washingtonpost.com/wp~srv/
   politics/special/affirm/stories/aa110497.htm>.

Bradley, Bill. "Ending Racism Can Never Be Just About
   Numbers." *Los Angeles Times* 15 Jan. 1996: B5. Electric Library. 17 Sep. 1996
   <http://www.elibrary.com>.

Dickerson, M. "Affirmative Action Opponents: Class-Based
   Help Would Do More." Gannett News Service 1 Apr.
   1995: 10 pars. 10 Aug. 1996
   <http://www.elibrary.com>.

Goodwin, M.E. "An Obituary to Affirmative Action and a
   Call for Self-Reliance." ERIC Document Reproduction
   Service (1992). 2 Feb. 1996 CD-ROM. No. ED357998.

Greenman, Ted. "Studies Against Affirmative Action and
   for Equality." 29 Aug. 1996. 17 Sep. 1996
   <http://www.cwo.com/~tag/saae.html>.

Hopwood v. State of Texas v. Thurgood Marshall Legal
   Society and Black Pre-Law Association. 94-50569 (18
   Mar. 1996) 24 Dec. 1998 <http://www.ljx.com/
   topdecision/dec0409.html>.

Jachik, S., and Lederman, D. "Appeals Court Bars Racial
   Preference in College Admissions." *Chronicle of
   Higher Education* 42 (1995): 26-29.

Kahlenberg, Richard. "Class, Not Race." *New Republic* 3
    Apr. 1995: 21–27.
Kemp, Jack. "Affirmative Action: The 'Racial Republican'
    Example." *Post* [Cincinnati] 24 Aug. 1995: PG. Elec-
    tric Library 10 Sep. 1996 <http://www.elibrary.com>.
Lappe, Frances Moore. *Rediscovering America's Values*.
    New York: Ballantine Books, 1989.
Lopez, Gretchen E. "Beyond Zero-Sum Diversity: Student
    Support for Educational Equity." *Educational Record*
    76.1 (1995): 55–62. ERIC Document Reproduction Ser-
    vice. 1 Oct 1996 CD-ROM. No. EJ 508623.
Noguera, Pedro. "A Popular Movement for Social Justice."
    In Motion Magazine (1996): 20 par. 12 Apr. 1996
    <http://www.inmotionmagazine.com/pedro2.html>.
Online NewsHour. "Color-Blind Justice." 1 July 1996 24
    Dec. 1998 <http://www.pbs.org/newshour/bb/law/
    july96/scotus_7-1.html>.
Rockwell, Paul. "Angry White Guys for Affirmative
    Action," 17 Apr. 1996: 11 par.
    <http://www.inmotionmagazine.com//press.html>.
Sanchez, Claudio. "Future of Affirmative Action in Higher
    Education." *National Public Radio* 13 January 1996:
    9 pars. Electric Library, p. B5 1 Oct. 1996
    <http://www.elibrary.com>.
S.B. 1419, Texas State Legislature. (1997) 31 Dec. 1998
    <http://www.capitol2.tlc.state.tx.us:8888>.
University of California Regents v. Bakke, 438 U.S. 265
    (1978) 24 Dec. 1998 <http://caselaw.findlaw.com>.
"University of Texas Drops Automatic Admissions Policy."
    Valley Morning Star 9 June 1996: C7.

NOTE: Whenever you see a long URL with **cgi** in it, do not cite anything including and after the indicator **cgi**. In the University of California Regents v. Bakke citation above, the entire URL when this item was located on the Web was: <http://caselaw.findlaw.com/cgi-bin/getcase. p1?court=US&vol=438&invol=265>. Everything including and following cgi is a temporary address generated by a search engine. If you return to that address, you will not find your original source. In the Bakke example, by leaving out the temporary address generated by the search engine, the person wanting to find the court case will go to the site where the case is located. The user will have to locate the specific court case by following the steps indicated by the specific site.

APA Style Title Page

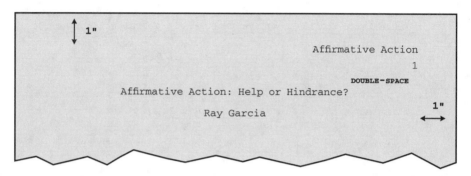

APA Style Abstract Page

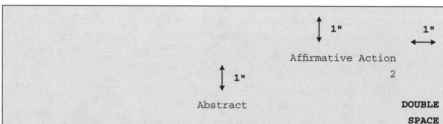

APA Style First Page

1"

Affirmative Action

1"

3

DOUBLE SPACE

Affirmative Action: Help or Hindrance?

At a recent "Day of Conversations" about diversity
on my campus, I found myself disagreeing with both faculty and other students on whether affirmative action in
university admission policies was beneficial or harmful.
This experience led me to realize that I needed to
explore affirmative action in greater depth. I wanted to
learn whether the lukewarm attitude toward affirmative
action and diversity issues at my campus was justified
and whether the nation's policies toward affirmative
action had changed. What is the current status of affirmative action programs nationally? Have the courts
changed their attitudes toward affirmative action? And if
affirmative action programs in their current form are
being threatened by legislation and court decisions, are
there any viable alternatives for reducing discrimination in admission policies and promoting diversity among
the student body?

Some background about the history of affirmative
action may be helpful. Affirmative action is a series of
programs put into place during Lyndon Johnson's presi-
dency, programs that were designed to correct inequities
in college enrollments based upon previous disadvantages
that minorities as groups had experienced. The arguments
in favor of affirmative action stress the need to remedy
the effects of past discrimination against minorities
and women. These remedies include:

DOUBLE
SPACE

1"

1"

APA Style—References List

References

Achieving faculty diversity: debunking the myths. (1997,
    February). *Diversity Digest*. Available:
    http:www.inform.umd.edu/diversityweb/Digest/F97/
    research.html [1998, December 24].

Alicea, I. P. (1995). Dismantling affirmative action.
    Journal of Blacks in Higher Education, 5 (19), 4.

Banks, R. R. (1995, May 22). Race matters most. *Los
    Angeles Times*. Available: http:www.elibrary.com
    [1998, December 23].

Barnes, J. E. (1997, November 17). Houston slows the
    tidal wave. *U.S. News*. Available:
    http://www.usnews.com/usnews/issue/971117afi.htm
    [1999, January 5].

Biskupic, J. (1997, November 4). Affirmative action ban
    is left intact by supreme court. *Washington Post*.
    Available: http:www.washingtonpost.com/wp-srv/
    politics/special/affirm/stories/aa110497.htm [1998,
    December 24].

Bradley, B. (1996, September 17). Ending racism can
    never be just about numbers. *Los Angeles Times*.
    Available: http://www.elibrary.com [1999, January
    5].

Color-blind justice. (1996, July 1). Online NewsHour.
    Available: http://www.pbs.org/newshour/bb/law/
    july96/scotus_7-1.html [1998, December 24].

Dickerson, M. (1995, April 1). Affirmative action oppo-
    nents: class-based help would do more. *Gannett News
    Service*. Available: http://www.elibrary.com [1999,
    January 4].

Goodwin, M. E. (1992). An obituary to affirmative action and a call for self-reliance. *ERIC Document Service*. Available: CD-ROM No. ED357998.

Greenman, T. (1996, August 29). Students against affirmative action and for equality. Available: http:www.cwo.com/~tag/saae.html [1998, December 23].

Hopwood v. state of texas v. thurgood marshall legal society and black pre-law association 94-50569. (1996, March 18). Available: http://www.lawnewsnetwork.com/topdecision/dec0409.html [1998, December 24].

Jachik, S., & Lederman, D. (1995). Appeals court bars racial preference in college admissions. *Chronicle of Higher Education* 42, 26-29.

Kahlenberg, R. (1995, April 3). Class, not race. *New Republic* 212, 21-27.

Kemp, J. (1995, August 24). Affirmative action: the "radical republican" example. *Post* [Cincinnati], *PG Electric Library*. Available: http://www.elibrary.com [1999, January 3].

Lappe, F. M. (1989). *Rediscovering America's Values*. New York: Ballantine Books.

Lopez, G. E. (1995). Beyond zero-sum diversity: student support for educational equity. *Educational Record* 76 (1), 55-62. Available: ERIC Document Reproduction Service, CD ROM No. EJ508623.

Noguera, P. (1996). A popular movement for social justice. *In Motion Magazine*. Available: http://www.inmotionmagazine.com/pedro2.html [1998, December 23].

Rockwell, P. (1996, April 17). Angry white guys for affirmative action. *In Motion Magazine*. Available: http://www.inmotionmagazine.com/press.html [1999, January 3].

Sanchez, C. (1996, January 13). Future of affirmative action in higher education. *National Public Radio*. Available: http://www.elibrary.com [1998, December 22].

S. B. 1419. (1997). *Texas State Legislature*. Available: http://capitol2.tlc.state.tx.us:8888 [1998, December 31].

University of California Regents v. Bakke, 438 U.S. 265 (1978). Available: http://caselaw.findlaw.com [1998, December 24].

University of Texas Drops Automatic Admissions Policy. (1996, June 9). *Valley Morning Star* C7.

Note: Whenever you see a long URL with **cgi** in it, do not cite anything including and after the indicator **cgi**. In the University of California Regents v. Bakke citation above, the entire URL when we located this item on the Web was: http://caselaw.findlaw.com/cgi-bin/getcase.pl?court=US&vol=438&invol=265. Everything including and following cgi is a temporary address generated by a search engine. If you return to that address, you will not find your original source. In the Bakke example, by leaving out the temporary address generated by the search engine, the person wanting to find the court case will get to the site where the case is located. The user will have to locate the specific court case by following the steps indicated by the specific site.

EXPLORING CITATION PROBLEMS

The Web poses new problems for researchers. As you know if you have visited the same Web site several times, the content can change, sometimes daily. In the past, someone who wanted to check the sources in a research paper could access the very same source that the writer used. With the Web, it is almost impossible to be sure that your reader will have access to the identical information you have.

There are other problems, too. The addresses for sites change. It may be that when your readers type in the URL that you provided in a research paper they will get a message indicating that there is no known URL with that address.

Another problem is the information at each site varies and may not fit the models in this or other style guides. What should you do? Create your own format if the sites you want to document do not fit the examples. Web sites vary so much that no style manual could ever anticipate all the variants you will find. Try to imitate the basic structure of the citation as much as you can. As long as your teacher knows that you have followed the general pattern, and you are consistent, you need not worry about whether you are right or not. With the Web, no one can anticipate all the varieties of citation problems that will occur.

Still another problem students report is the use of angle brackets (< >). If you try to type angle brackets using Microsoft Word, the default setting in the program removes them and turns the URL into a hyperlink. If you want to remove that setting, click on the Tools menu bar and select AutoCorrect, then select AutoFormat as you type. Under "Replace as You Type," remove the check from "internet and network paths with hyperlinks."

Finally, there is a logistical problem. It is not easy to keep track of URLs. Some browsers do not show the URL of the page you are viewing. Most sites do not include the URL on the page itself. Thus, if you save a Web page to disk thinking that you have got your information intact, you may discover later that you do not have the URL. It is easy to do a Web search on your topic and find the URL—far easier than running back to the library and taking a book out again—but it is a problem that you can avoid if you are careful. Here are some suggestions:

■ Save the file with the name of the URL.
■ Open files as soon as you save them and copy the URL into them.
■ If you print pages immediately rather than save them to disk, check to see if Netscape now automatically prints the title of the file. Netscape places the URL in the header of each page.

Here is a general form you might use to keep track of online sources you plan to cite in your paper:

AUTHOR	DATE	TITLE	AVAILABILITY	ACCESS

PRACTICE BOX

1. Discuss the importance of being able to track down a specific site. Do some teachers and scholars pay excessive attention to tracking sources? Consider the following example of how an author uses excessive detail in a citation: Why is it so important, in this person's opinion, to have all the detail?

   > Vail, E. <Esther.Vail@p15.f333.n2613.z1.fidonet.org>, Reynolds, L. <vog@rain.org>, and Taibi, Solomon <taibi@ix.netcom.com>. 'Middle Names Part II'. Articles <814840481.AA.00152@rochgte.fidonet.org>, <46s2s1$k55@news.rain.org>, <46s701$8tf@ixnews4.ix.netcom.com> and <46t4m5$2jp@cr110.crl.com>, in : USENET newsgroup alt.usage.english

   The author of this citation explains her view:

   > It is possible to omit them [the long codes for articles] considering the ephemeral nature of news articles. However, bear in mind that it is already sometimes possible, and will in the future be increasingly so, to look up articles in news archives (see, for example, <http://www.dejanews.com>), so it is usually better to include them.

2. There is considerable difference of opinion among scholars as to the format of electronic sources. Melvin Page, a history professor, believes that URLs should begin on a new line so that the text can be easily converted to HTML documents. Should citation format vary so much from one discipline to another?

3. Gather a list of sources for a project you are working on. With a partner, write them in correct electronic citation format. In small groups, review your work. As you begin writing citations for Web sources, you'll discover many difficulties, since Web resources are so varied. In all likelihood, you'll find that you have to "create" ways of citing some of your sources. See if you can come to some agreement on the most appropriate way to format your citations.

COPYRIGHT CONSIDERATIONS

In addition to knowing how to document sources, you need to understand copyright laws. The term *copyright* refers to protection provided to authors for their "copy"—whether a printed text, a movie, a visual, or a recording. From 1978 on, copyright protection has been automatic, and a simple statement such as "this document cannot be distributed in its entirety without permission of the author" is all that you have to do to guarantee your authorial rights. Also, include a copyright symbol © and the date. (Such a statement is not absolutely necessary but it can prevent accidental misuse by others.)

Before the Web, students rarely had to worry about copyright laws. The few lines of text from books or journals that are included in student papers are within the "fair use" length guidelines. (You can quote up to 300 words from a book or 150 words from a magazine or newspaper, if the total you quote is not more than 20 percent of the original.) But if you link a source on the Web to your text, you can be considered to be "distributing" that source. It is always advisable to get permission to link to a given site. Most importantly, if you are writing a hypertext research paper that includes links to copyright-protected essays or poems that you have photocopied and included in an Appendix to your research project, do not scan the text into the computer and link it to your writing without receiving permission from the author. If you do, you may be guilty of copyright infringement.

CONCLUSION

Citation conventions for print-based sources have been set in place for years; Internet citation style, however, is still evolving. When you use the Web for research, you should continue using the same processes for citing sources that you have always used; but it *is* essential that these processes be adapted to Internet-specific needs of readers. Clearly, it is not always easy or even possible for a reader of an Internet-based research paper to track a source. But it is important that you, as a writer, do your best to provide clear and accurate guidelines for your readers.

If you have some doubts, include an explanatory footnote in which you let your reader know the context: for example, you may find that a given source that you found at a specific Web site is no longer there. If that is the case, use the source if you feel it is critical to your point, but be honest with your reader.

Above all, continue using the Internet for research. Do not let concerns about validity and citation questions stop you from including the results of your Internet-based research into your finished paper.

EXERCISES

1. Working from your note cards, develop a bibliography (Works Cited for MLA; References for APA) for your paper. Use the citation generator available at the companion Web site for this book to assist you.

2. Working in groups, review drafts of one another's papers. Use questions such as the following to guide you:

   a.   Is there an appropriate balance between the writer's perspective and the information and opinions gathered from your sources, or is the paper simply a collection of quotes, paraphrases, and summaries?

   b.   Are the writer's points supported with sufficient evidence from outside sources?

   c.   As far as you can tell, has the writer used valid sources to support his or her points?

   d.   Has the writer varied the way he or she introduces quotes?

3. Return to the latest draft of your paper and make sure you have used correct internal citation style. Check the items such as the following: (1) Have you listed page numbers for direct quotations and paraphrased passages? (2) If you have not mentioned the author in your sentence, have you included the name of the author or authors in the parenthetic citation?

Appendix:
Internet Basics

What Is the Internet?

The Internet consists of a worldwide collection of interconnected servers—computers with stores of information that are kept running at all times. Individual computers connect to the Internet in different ways, through regular telephone lines, high-speed telephone lines (ISDN lines), cable television networks, and campuswide or corporate networks. Sometimes the server's information is accessible to users free of charge, such as is the case in most colleges and universities, which provide e-mail and Web access to students and faculty. Other times the server is owned by a company such as America Online or CompuServ or one of the thousands of Internet Service Providers (ISPs) that charge a monthly fee to access the World Wide Web and other information.

Information on these servers was developed in many ways: by individuals, by companies, and by institutions. Anyone can publish a Web page as long as he or she has an account on a server that is connected to the Internet. Some information, such as that developed by government agencies, museums, educational institutions, or libraries is of high quality. Other information, sometimes made available by for-profit businesses or organizations, is biased and often inferior in quality. Still other information, posted by individuals, may be valuable or useless. It is up to each user to evaluate and determine the quality of each page.

What Is the World Wide Web?

The World Wide Web is the portion of the Internet that has been developed in hypertext format. Hypertext documents allow users to move from one topic to another by clicking the underlined or specially colored word that, when clicked, connects you to either another document (at the same or another site) or to another portion of the document. Web links have been coded in the text using Hypertext Markup Language (HTML).

Until a few years ago, hypertext resources constituted just a small share of the information on the entire Internet. Today, the World Wide Web is almost synonymous with the term Internet, since even nonhypertext Internet sites are now accessible through the Web. Internet areas such as Gopher sites, FTP sites, and Telnet sites are now accessible through Web browsers. If you are connected to the Web, you are connected to the Internet too.

The information resources available on the World Wide Web consist of a wide range of material: digital versions of traditional library information along with totally new kinds of information, ranging from image collections and online museums to collections of rare books that have been scanned and made available to larger numbers of people than would otherwise have had access to them.

Frequently Asked Questions (FAQs)

What is a home page? The term *home page* is used to refer to the first page in a set of pages or screens of information. The home page often functions as an index to the information available at a given Web site. For example, most colleges have home pages with pointers to many places on campus, such as the library and department offices, as well as to information resources, such as campus events and online directories. Each page connected to the home page—the library page, for example—lists information about its own resources along with links to related pages across the world. Each home page has its own Internet address or Universal Resource Locator (URL), which describes the exact location of the starting page along with the computer on which it is stored.

This book has its own home page <http://www.prenhall.com/rodrigues> which is stored at the Prentice Hall Web site. Visit this site to review concepts in this text as well as to locate supplemental information.

If you want to place information on the Web, you need to put it on either your own home page or on someone else's page. To make it available to the Internet community, your page needs to be "published" on the Web. That means that you (or someone else) need to have an account on a computer that is connected to the Web, and that account must provide you with enough disk space for your home page and any related pages.

What is a browser? A browser is a software program (such as Netscape Navigator or Windows Explorer) that lets you view the contents of the Web. Browsers are designed to enable a user to jump from one Web location to another. Browsers also allow you to access non-Web information on the Internet, such as software downloads at FTP sites or Gopher sites, which still contain much valuable information that has not yet been transformed into hypertext.

The same Web page may look different with different browsers. That is because the developers of the Web, researchers in Switzerland, created a method for sharing text that allowed it to be viewed on both high-end and low-end computers. They developed Hypertext Markup Language (HTML), a system for marking up pages with code to indicate how each page should be displayed on the computer screen and where on the page each element should be positioned. Even though a Web page looks different on different machines, the source code is the same. The code is hidden from your view, but it can be revealed by clicking on **View,** then clicking on **Source** (in Netscape).

What is a URL? Each site on the Web and each page on each site has a unique address or location. That address is called a Universal Resource Locator, or URL. Entering a Web address correctly into the location panel of a browser allows you to access a specific site and specific information (a specific page) at that site. Depending on how the page has been "marked up" (with HTML), you can also access a specific part of a given part of a page.

How are Web sites named? Sites on the Web follow elaborate schemes: All computers have an organization name and a domain suffix that indicates what kind of computer is hosting the information—a government computer, a computer at an educational institution, a military computer, or a computer at a nonprofit organization.

How Are Web Sites Developed?

The Web is a democratic place: the information placed on it has been developed by all kinds of people, including students in K–12 and college classes. Everyone has an opportunity to contribute to the Web's growing body of resources. Many Web sites are intentionally designed to encourage collaboration. For example, the home page of the Internet Public Library includes this message: "If you'd like to suggest a resource to be added to this collection, please fill out our Recommendation form."

You might want to develop your own Web page or a collection of pages. If you want to contribute information to the Website for this text, please send an e-mail message to <drodrigues@utb1.utb.edu>. Your class pages, individual sample essays, or class magazines will be added to a list of links for this chapter.

Despite the democratic spirit of much of the Web, a growing number of Web sites are not available to the public. To access resources such as the *Encyclopaedia Britannica* and other proprietary reference tools or databases, you or your institution must first pay a subscription fee. Many people feel strongly that information resources should be made available to everyone free of charge (much as they are in public libraries). As a result, volunteers are attempting to develop free substitutes for many proprietary information resources. For example, *The Free Encyclopedia* has been developed by a team of volunteers. The only problem with this kind of information is that it is not necessarily reliable (that is, the entries may not have been checked for validity), whereas copyright-protected encyclopedias undergo a rigorous review and editing process.

If you have not yet explored the Web extensively, you may be surprised to discover that many sites feature a label that reads "under construction." The developers want you to understand that what you see is only a draft of what they hope their home page will eventually become. In actuality, all sites are continually under construction and reconstruction. What you see one day of the week may be different from what you see the next day. Unlike a printed resource that often takes a long time to be published, Web sites can be published and revised at a moment's notice. They can disappear just as quickly; thus you should save a copy of all pages that you use as sources for your research paper.

Glossary

Bandwidth Term of measurement for width of Internet cables. Wider bandwidths allow more data to pass through them.

Bauds per second (bps) The rate at which data passes through a modem.

Bibliographic records A record is a set of information that is stored as a unit. A bibliographic record contains publication information.

Bibliography A list of sources used in a research paper or any list of sources about a given topic, including books, articles, and online sources.

Boolean searching Searching that is based on the logical principles set forth by mathematician George Boole. If you want to find many sources on your topic, you can use two synonyms for your topic combined with OR (e.g., technology OR distance education). If you want to limit the number of sources you find, you should use AND. (Technology AND distance education would result in only those sources that use both terms.)

Browser A software program designed to allow users to explore the World Wide Web.

Call number A number found on the spine of a book or collection of documents used by libraries so that specific resources can be easily found.

Cataloging software Software used to organize a library's holdings.

CD-ROM Storage medium for computer data.

Chat areas Web or other Internet sites where individuals "chat" by typing messages to one another. Chat areas are usually focused on a specific topic.

Citation The information in a bibliographic entry that allows a reader to locate the same source that the writer used.

Current periodicals The most recent issues of periodicals that are usually found in open stacks. When they are no longer current, they are bound by volume and shelved elsewhere.

Database Software designed to allow a user to enter information into categories in such a way that it can be sorted and retrieved at a later date.

Descriptors Keywords from the text of an article used when storing information in a database or when retrieving information.

Digital age Term used to refer to the information age or age of technology as opposed to the age of print or the age of books.

Digitize To turn a picture or a printed page into a computer format that allows the data to be transformed.

Digitized photographs Photographs that have been put on disk and that can be resized or edited.

Directory Groups of files stored together. Similar to folders and subfolders in Macintosh and Windows environments.

Disc Sometimes spelled *disk* or *diskette,* this term usually refers to a floppy disk (either 5¼" or 3½").

Domain suffix The domain is the place where your Internet service originates. The suffix is the end portion of an Internet address that indicates the nature of your site. For example, **edu** indicates an educational site, whereas **gov** indicates a unit of government.

Download Term used for the procedure of moving information from a remote computer to your own computer.

E-journals Articles collected together on Internet sites. Sometimes these journals are "refereed" (sent out to reviewers in the field before acceptance). Web journals are typically done in hypertext format.

E-mail Method of communicating with others by sending messages from one computer address to another.

E-mail address The unique set of letters followed by a computer's location name that is provided to you so that you can send and receive messages across the Internet.

Electronic sources Sources that are in nonprint media.

Eudora E-mail program available in Macintosh or IBM-compatible versions.

Folder Metaphor for an area on a computer where individual files (and other folders) are stored.

FTP File transfer protocol. The standard way of getting files from a remote computer and putting them on your computer or of putting files from your computer on the remote machine.

Genre bibliography A list of sources in a specific genre, such as the novel, short story, drama, essay, or poetry.

Gopher Menu-based software designed to interact with other computers running similar software.

Gopher interface The screen design or way of enabling users to access information on the Gopher system. Gopher uses a treelike system to organize information into files and folders.

Graphical interface A computer screen display that enables a user to point and click to select information and navigate the program. On the Web, it is a way of providing access to information through pages that are designed with attractive text and images, some portions of which are linked to other Web pages through hypertext links.

Hit A match between a search term and a word in one of the titles or texts that are in the database.

Home page The starting "page" or the first screen in a set of Web pages. Each home page has links to many other pages either at the current site or at other locations.

HTML Hypertext Markup Language—the way of coding text, images, and other digitized files to make them accessible through the Web.

HTTP Hypertext Transfer Protocol—the set of standards for transmitting data on the Web.

Hypertext Text that includes links to other text or images, usually accessible by clicking on underlined words or phrases in the initial document.

Images Pictures or drawings that have been digitized and stored on a computer.

Information resources Computer-accessible books, journals, pictures, audio files, etc., that can be retrieved via the Internet.

Interactive forums Discussion or chat software accessible through Web sites. Messages are stored for easy reading and responding.

Interface The part of the computer screen design that suggests ways of navigating the program.

Interlibrary loan The process of ordering a library item from another library when your local library does not own it.

Internet Worldwide network of networks, including Gopher sites, Web sites, and FTP sites.

Interview A process of asking questions of individuals. Check the style guide you are using to determine the proper citation style for interviews.

Keywords Words related to a given topic used to locate information on that topic in a database.

Launch Term used to start an application such as Telnet or FTP.

List server Computer used to administer and organize mailing lists. Two popular mailing list programs that run on list servers are LISTPROC and LISTSERV.

Location box Place in the Netscape screen that displays the address of the Internet site currently being viewed.

Login or Log in When you log in to a computer you identify yourself to the computer so that it can check to see if you are an authorized user. Typically, you need both a **login name** and a **password** to identify yourself with a computer.

Login name   The set of letters and/or numbers used to identify yourself to the computer. This name is often used as part of your e-mail address.

Login prompt   Typically, the word "login:" appears on the screen of a computer that requires an access code, as a way of "prompting" or reminding you of what you need to do next. In this case, a login prompt indicates that you need to enter your **login name** and press <Enter>.

Lynx   A text-based Web browser that runs on the UNIX operating system. To use Lynx, you typically need to have access to a UNIX computer at your campus or workplace. DOS versions of Lynx are also available, but not common.

Main menu   The opening list of selections on a given program.

Menu   A list of selections that appears on the opening screen of a program or on a subsection of a program.

Microform   A type of film or paper that contains information in a miniaturized form, such as microfiche or microfilm, that requires a special machine to read it.

Modem   Device used to translate computer data into a format that can be sent through standard telephone lines. *Modem* stands for modulator-demodulator.

Netscape   Graphical browser that integrates newsgroups, mail, FTP, Gopher, and Web access into a common program.

Newsgroup   Discussion groups on various topics, accessible through a browser or through special software called newsreaders or through Internet sites that provide public access to newsgroups.

Online   Term used to refer to information available on the Internet.

Online catalog   A catalog that is contained in a computer database in the library.

Online source   A source that can be accessed on the Internet.

Operators   Terms used to describe AND, OR, and NOT when used to separate keywords in a search. Each of these terms directs the way the search "operates." Also called Boolean operators. See **Boolean searching.**

Packets   Clusters of computer data that are coded at transmission and decoded at the destination.

Password   Secret way of identifying yourself to a computer on which you have an account. The **login name** is the public way you identify yourself to the computer.

Path   The location of files is frequently referred to by giving its "path" or place in a **directory** structure. For example, if a file named "book.txt" is stored in a subdirectory of a directory called "pub," its path would be /pub/book.txt. Longer paths indicate deeper directory and subdirectory structures.

Periodical   A journal, magazine, or newspaper. Periodicals are also called *serials*.

Periodical article   An article published in a journal, magazine, or newspaper.

Periodical index   A listing of all articles published in journals, magazines, or newspapers. There are different types of periodical indexes, each specializing in a broad category, such as magazine articles.

Post   To send a message on e-mail to a mailing list or to a newsgroup.

PPP   Point-to-point protocol (agreed-on standard). Method of transferring Internet data from one point to another.

Query   To request information by inserting search terms into a database.

Records   Sets of information stored in a database.

Remote site   Any place away from the location of your computer. If you can log in to your computer from another location, then you are said to have remote access.

Screen   The visual information that appears on your computer monitor. Depending on the size of the computer monitor, a screen can hold less than a page or several pages of text.

Search engine   Computer program designed to look through massive amounts of information in a database and retrieve a list of resources that match your **query.**

Search form   The area on the search tool where you enter the **keyword**s and other information needed to perform a search.

Search screen   The image that appears on your computer when you indicate to a **search tool** that you would like to perform a search.

Search tool   Computer program used for searching a database, sometimes including various categories of information that can be searched along with a **search engine.**

Service provider   A company that provides Internet "service" or access.

Shell   A program allowing limited access to a UNIX computer.

Site   Computer location that offers specific directories and subdirectories of information accessible through Internet browsers or through such programs as **Gopher** or **FTP.**

Source code   The set of commands that tells your browser how to display a page on your computer screen.

Subject heading   A term in a library database or reference that categorizes items that are similar to one another.

Supercomputers   Extremely powerful computers used primarily by scientists and often shared with others who log in from remote sites.

Surfing   Term used to describe the act of moving rapidly from site to site on the Web.

Survey   A research technique for asking questions of a particular group of people. It may be written or recorded. Interviews must be cited in your Works Cited or Reference section.

Telnet Term coined from the words "telephone" and "network." Telnet software enables you to use phone lines or other Internet lines to log in to computers at other sites around the world, provided that you have a **login name** and a **password.**

Terminal A monitor and keyboard that interacts with another computer. When you **log in** to computers at remote sites, your computer becomes nothing more than a terminal or transfer device for viewing or interacting with information on the remote computer.

Text-based interface A computer screen display that requires a user to type commands rather than use a mouse to point and click to select actions. When you Telnet to an Internet site (such as a library), you are in a text-based environment rather than a graphical one.

Transfer files To move files from one computer to another, usually using software such as Xmodem or Kermit.

Uniform Resource Locator The URL or address for an Internet site.

URL Uniform Resource Locator or address for an Internet site.

Usenet Bulletin board system designed in the 1970s by computer scientists, which is now used for newsgroups or discussion groups by individuals everywhere.

WAIS Wide Area Information System—a software package that enables multiple databases at remote sites to be searched using the same query system.

Web interface A way of accessing information through the graphical kind of screen typical of the Web.

Web page Units of information one or more screens in length, but often no longer than one or two pages. Web pages are linked together with anchors that allow you to jump from one to the other.

Web site Location of a computer called a server that contains the home pages for your company, department, or group.

World Wide Web That portion of the Internet that has been formatted with hypertext links. These links can be text files, audio files, graphic images, or video.

Z39.50 Protocol used by librarians to organize and code their catalog information in such a way that allows it to be searched with a common **search form.**

Zine Term coined from maga*zine* to refer to the many collections of essays or samples of creative writing that are made available on the Internet.

Works Cited

American Library Association. Anglo-American Cataloguing Rules, 2nd ed. ALA: Champaign-Urbana, 1988.

"Books, Websites, or Journal? The Information Cycle," SUNY Farmingdale Greenley Library Reference Department. 12 June 1999 <http://www.farmingdale.edu/campuspages/computingandlibrary/library/inflow.html>.

Day, Michael. "Writing in the Matrix: Students Tapping the Living Database on the Computer Network" in *The Dialogic Classroom* by Galin and Latchaw (eds.). NCTE: Urbana, IL, 1998. 43–66.

Dobler, Bruce, and Harry Bloomberg. "How Much Web Would a Web Course Weave If a Web Course Would Weave Webs?" in *The Dialogic Classroom* by Galin and Latchaw. NCTE: Urbana, IL, 1998. 151–173.

Franklin, Phyllis. "Footnotes in the Electronics Age," *USA Today* 6 February 1996: D7.

Galin, Jeff, and Joan Latchaw, eds. *The Dialogic Classroom*. NCTE: Urbana, IL, 1998.

Jacobson, Robert L. "Researchers Temper Their Ambitions for Digital Libraries," *The Chronicle of Higher Education* 24 November 1995: A19.

Jones, Steven G., ed. *Cybersociety: Computer Mediated Communication and Community*. Sage: Thousand Oaks, CA, 1995.

Kling, Ron, and Lisa Covi. "Electronic Journals and Legitimate Media in the Systems of Scholarly Publishing." The Information Society. 1995: 11 (4). 26 Apr. 99 <http://www.chass.utoronto.ca/epc/chwp/kling/index.html.>.

Li, Xia, and Nancy Crane. *Electronic Style: An Expanded Guide to Citing Electronic Information*. 2nd ed. Information Today: Medford, NJ, 1996.

Macrorie, Ken. *Searching Writing*. Hayden: Rochelle Park, NJ, 1980.

Rocklin, Tom. "Where Does the Time Go? Another Demand Brought on by Technology" in *Academic Leader*, Sample Issue, p. 1 N.D.

Smock, Raymond W. "What Promise Does the Internet Hold for Scholars?" *The Chronicle of Higher Education,* 22 September 1995: B1.

Tennant, Roy. "The Best Tools for Searching the Internet," *Syllabus* 9 (5) 1996: 36–38.

Zimmerman, Don, and Dawn Rodrigues. *Researching Writing in the Disciplines.* Harcourt, Brace, Jovanovich: New York, 1993.

Figure Acknowledgments

CHAPTER 1

Figure 1.1   E-commerce Web site. Copyright 1999 internet.com LLC

Figure 1.2   Books on E-commerce in Rutgers Library. Reprinted, by permission, from The Rutgers University Libraries Information System Library

CHAPTER 2

Figure 2.1   Home page for library at the University of Texas at Brownsville. Reprinted, by permission, from Arnulfo Oliviera Library of the University of Texas at Brownsville and Texas Southmost College

Figure 2.3   Netscape Navigator with navigation bar and location bar. Reprinted, by permission, from the Colorado State University Libraries online catalog which uses Innovative Interfaces, Inc. Software. Portions copyright Netscape Communications Corporation, 1998. All rights reserved. Netscape, Netscape Navigator, and the Netscape N logo are registered trademarks of Netscape in the United States and other countries.

Figure 2.4   Beaucoup Search page. Copyright 1999 beaucoup.com.

CHAPTER 3

Figure 3.1   Catalogs and indexes in the Berkeley Digital Library. Reprinted, by permission, from the Berkeley Digital Library Sun SITE

Figure 3.4   Journals and newsletters on the Web. Reprinted, by permission, from the Jean and Alexander Heard Libraries of Vanderbilt University

CHAPTER 4

Figure 4.1   Results of search for database in Sociology. Reprinted, by permission, from the University of Illinois at Urbana-Champaign Library.

Figure 4.2   Results of search for subject-area guides. Alta Vista and the Alta Vista logo are trademarks or service marks of the Alta Vista Company. Used with permission.

Figure 4.3   Results of search for electronic commerce. Copyright 1999 internet.com LLC.

CHAPTER 6

Figure 6.1   The attachment box within Netscape Mail. Portions copyright Netscape Communications Corporation, 1998. All rights reserved. Netscape, Netscape Navigator, and the Netscape N logo are registered trademarks of Netscape in the United States and other countries.

CHAPTER 7

Figure 7.1   Example of a personal set of bookmark folders. Portions copyright Netscape Communications Corporation, 1998. All rights reserved. Netscape, Netscape Navigator, and the Netscape N logo are registered trademarks of Netscape in the United States and other countries.

Figure 7.2   Example of a set of brainstormed bookmark folders and subfolders at the early stage of collecting and bookmarking possible sources for a research project. Portions copyright Netscape Communications Corporation, 1998. All rights reserved. Netscape, Netscape Navigator, and the Netscape N logo are registered trademarks of Netscape in the United States and other countries.

Figure 7.3   Examples of subfolders within subfolders as the researcher develops categories for filing bookmarks. Portions copyright Netscape Communications Corporation, 1998. All rights reserved. Netscape, Netscape Navigator, and the Netscape N logo are registered trademarks of Netscape in the United States and other countries.

Figure 7.4   Example of an annotation for a bookmark. Portions copyright Netscape Communications Corporation, 1998. All rights reserved. Netscape, Netscape Navigator, and the Netscape N logo are registered trademarks of Netscape in the United States and other countries.

Figure 7.5   Example of an electronic workspace. Portions copyright Netscape Communications Corporation, 1998. All rights reserved. Netscape, Netscape Navigator, and the Netscape N logo are registered trademarks of Netscape in the United States and other countries.

Figure 7.6   Example of a research notebook directory (a log kept as the research proceeds). Portions copyright Netscape Communications Corporation, 1998. All rights reserved. Netscape, Netscape Navigator, and the Netscape N logo are registered trademarks of Netscape in the United States and other countries.

Index